A PRACTICAL KEY TO THE KANNADA LANGUAGE

A
PRACTICAL KEY
TO THE
KANNADA LANGUAGE

REV. F. ZIEGLER

GYAN

Published by

Gyan Publishing House
5, Ansari Road
Daryaganj, New Delhi-110002
Phone: 011-47034999, 9811692060
E-mail: books@gyanbooks.com

Distribution Network
gyanbooks.com
India, USA, Canada, UK, Australia, France

ISBN : 978-81-212-3027-8 (PB)
First Published, 1953

2nd Impression 2020

Printed at: Gyan Press, Delhi.

A
Practical Key to the Kannada Language
Author: Rev. F. Ziegler

A PRACTICAL KEY

TO THE

KANARESE LANGUAGE

BY

F. ZIEGLER

MISSIONARY

SIXTH EDITION

PUBLISHED BY THE
BASEL MISSION BOOK DEPOT, MANGALORE
1953

INTRODUCTION

(Not to be turned over)

The manner in which Europeans, fresh from home, frequently set about learning an Indian language is somewhat like the following—They take a grammar and begin with the numerous characters of the foreign language; then they take some Primer or other book and learn to read. Eager to read by themselves, they do not like to let their Munshi read the words to them, pronouncing them after him, but try to pronounce them first, ordering the Munshi to correct their errors. But the Munshi, poor man, is afraid of incurring the Sahib's displeasure by correcting him too often. Perhaps he has even learned by experience that his pupil is not very fond of being corrected, and he soon gets tired of correcting him, permitting him to acquire a vicious pronunciation. Meanwhile the pupil exerts himself to learn the declensions and conjugations by heart, tries to translate his reading book, learning the words and phrases or even whole pages of the book by rote. But what are the fruits of his exertions? Most probably the following:

1. He gets a faulty pronunciation of which he can only rid himself afterwards with great trouble and loss of time, if at all.
2. He encumbers his memory with a multitude of words for which he has no immediate use, and which he soon forgets again.
3. His ear does not get accustomed to the peculiar sounds of the vernacular when spoken by a native.
4. Consequently it takes an exceedingly long time before he is able to converse freely with natives even on common subjects.

To prevent these drawbacks, we advise the student to adhere to the following rules:

I. Be careful to lay a sound foundation; therefore let every thing you learn be correct, making sure that it is so, and do not be satisfied unless you have a thorough knowledge of it.

II. Save time.

*I. To lay a sound foundation,**

1. You should *learn*, but should not attempt *to teach yourself;* you should not pronounce a single word, or put two words together by yourself.
2. To learn a sound or expression, you should repeat it hundreds, even thousands of times, not by yourself, but referring every time immediately to a correct standard, that is, a native.

* We here partly quote from an essay on this subject by Colonel A. Cotton, which we read in an Indian Periodical nearly thirty years ago.

A*

3. Learn only one thing at a time, and do not think that you will be able to master the character, the pronunciation, the meaning and the grammar of the foreign language all at the same time.

4. Take care to give your whole strength to the really essential parts of the subject.

5. Last, but not least, learn the language, not by the eye, but by the ear.

II. To save time,

1. Do not begin with learning the foreign character, for
   (1) You can learn the language without it and will perhaps never want it.
   (2) It is a most serious hindrance, absorbing a great deal of attention.
   (3) It can be learned in one-hundredth part of the time which would be consumed at first, if learned after you have mastered the spoken language.

2. Do not begin with reading books, such as Primers, Readers, tracts and the like, which are composed with a view entirely different from that which you have, and will burden your memory with words of which you can make no use, at least not at the outset.

This little book is compiled with a view of assisting the student in following the above mentioned rules, furnishing the materials with which he may begin his studies in a profitable way. It consists

1. of the alphabet with its transcription in English characters.
2. of a vocabulary of 162 words, such as are indispensable to the beginner.
3. of a collection of 1000 homely phrases and sentences, containing only the words of the vocabulary with their transcription in English letters accompanied by a verbal and a free translation.

Care has been taken to introduce those words in as many different grammatical forms as possible, to the effect that the student may acquire the elements of the grammar of the foreign language at the same time as he is learning its vocabulary.*

To use these materials, the student should employ a good Munshi, if he can get one. If not, any native who can read and has a good pronunciation will do; a knowledge of English is not necessary for him. He should first take this alphabet, that is, its English transcription, and with the help of his Munshi carefully learn the pronunciation of those sounds, which are foreign to his own tongue. Englishmen should be especially careful to acquire a correct

* To enable the student to better grasp the grammar of the Kanarese idiom, in the second edition the Conjugations and Declensions, as far as their knowledge is required for the understanding of the phrases and sentences, have been gradually introduced at the head of the paragraphs. The student will find it useful to commit these persons of grammar to memory, though this is not indispensable, since by committing the phrases and sentences to memory, he will get a knowledge of grammar as well.

pronunciation of the vowels and diphthongs, a, â, ei, ou, and to avoid pronouncing *a* like the English *a* in *bad* or *far*, the letter v also has difficulties for them. Germans, chiefly natives of Southern Germany, should take the greatest care to distinguish the hard (mute) letters k, č, ṭ, t, p, and their aspirates from the soft ones g, j, ḍ, d, b, and their aspirates. On the whole it must never be forgotten that nearly all the consonants, and some of the vowels too, have a pronunciation different from that of the corresponding letter in English as well as in German.

After this, let the student go through the vocabulary. The Munshi, sitting at a little distance with a book in his hand, pronounces the first word; after him the student pronounces; the teacher repeats, and the student again, always adding the English word immediately after the vernacular. This should be done at least five times, or oftener, till the Munshi is satisfied with the student's pronunciation. The second word is treated in the same manner then the third, and in this way, the whole vocabulary is gone through several times. When the student is tolerably familiar with the words, he should put down the book and go over them again in the same way several times without looking at the words, till he can pronounce every word, and knows the meaning of every word without the slightest hesitation. When this is accomplished he should proceed to the phrases and sentences, which should be gone through in the same way. At first he should repeat every word separately, about five times, with its exact meaning, proceeding as far as time and inclination permit him on the first day. Next day he should go through the same sentences again in the same manner, when he will probably get a little further. On the third day he may treat the sentences of the first day somewhat differently, reading the whole sentence together with its free translation about five times each; this day also a new batch of sentences may be commenced, which should be treated as a first. Thus every batch is first to be read on two successive days in such a way that each word is pronounced separately five times with its exact meaning, and then the whole sentence together with its free translation. In this way he should go through the whole set of sentences to the end of the book again and again, taking care never to pronounce a word, except immediately after, and immediately before hearing it pronounced by his Munshi, and continuing this study till every one of the sentences is as familiar to him as his own tongue. He should at first do it from the book, and afterwards without it. We would especially caution young missionaries who can give all their time to the study of the vernacular, against the fancy that they will gain anything by committing words or phrases to memory by themselves, independent of the Munshi, or by proceeding to new subjects before the old ones are thoroughly mastered, since almost all the knowledge acquired in this way at the beginning will prove eventually of little or no use to them. If it seem too tedious to them to be doing the same thing always, they may employ part of their time in learning the native character, without, however, using it as yet in reading. They may also employ their spare time in acquiring as much information as possible on the geography and history of India, its religions, castes, customs, etc., which branches of study are almost as necessary to them as a knowledge of the language.

Having mastered the whole book in the way described, but not before, the student may proceed to learn the Kanarese character and begin to read some of the books published in the vernacular.

ABBREVIATIONS

acc. = *accusative*
adj. = *adjective*
adv. = *adverb*
a. p. = *any person*
C. = *Coast and Mysore*
e. g. = *exempli gratia, for example*
f. = *feminine*
g. = *gender*
G. = *German*
h. = *having*
hon. = *honorific*
intr. = *intransitive*
m. = *masculine*
n. = *neuter*
p. = *person, or page*
pl. = *plural*
p. p. = *past participle*
pr. p. = *present participle*
rel. part. or p. = *relative participle*
S. = *Southern Mahratta*
sup. = *superiors*
v. p. = *verbal participle*

1. The Kanarese Alphabet.

Remark:—*We have omitted the pure Sanskrit letters which do not occur in the Vocabulary of this Book.*

a. Vowels ಸ್ವರಗಳು.

ಅ	a	*as* a *in* America, *or in the German*	kann
		sometimes as a *in* ,, ,,	hat
ಆ	â	a *in* father, *or* ,, ,, ,,	Gabe
ಇ	i	i ,, him, ,, ,, ,, ,,	bitter
ಈ	î	i ,, police, ,, ,, ,, ,,	Sieb
ಉ	u	u ,, put, ,, ,, ,, ,,	Butter
ಊ	û	u ,, rude, ,, ,, ,, ,,	Ruh
		or oo ,, too,	
ಎ	e	e ,, pen, ,, ,, ,, ,,	Ende
ಏ	ê	e ,, eh, ,, ,, ,, ,,	Heer
		sometimes as e ,, there, ,, ,, ,, ,,	wer
ಐ	ei	ei ,, height, ,, ,, ,, ,,	Weib

Englishmen should take care not to pronounce the first part of this diphthong too open; it is not like the Italian "a", but rather like the short sound of "u" in *but.*

ಒ	o	*as* o *in* police, *or in the German*	Spott

It is the sound of "o" in *open* shortened, but not the common English short "o" as in *not*.

ಓ	ô	*as* o *in* noto, *or in the German*	rot
ಔ	ou	ou ,, out, ,, au ,, ,,	sauer

The vowels e and ê, when beginning a word, are spoken, and therefore transcribed like ye and yê, as in the English *yes* and *yea*; in the same way "o", when initial, is pronounced wo, and ô,, wô;[1] but when the word is closely united with the preceding one, the consonant sound disappears.

---

[1] To distinguish these vowel sounds from the true consonants "y" and "w" the former will be printed in italics: *y*, *w*.

b. Consonants ವ್ಯಂಜನಗಳು.

ಕ	k	*as* k *in* kick; *the German* k *without aspiration*	
ಖ	kh	k *aspirated, as*	,, ch in Chor
ಗ	g	*as* g *in* got, *or*	,, sagen; gehen
ಘ	gh	,, gh ,, Leghorn	
ಙ	ṅ	,, ng ,, sing	,, singen
ಚ	č	,, ch ,, child	,, deutsch, rutschen
ಛ	čh	ch *aspirated*	
ಜ	j	*as* j *in* jar	
ಝ	jh	jh *aspirated*	

The two sounds č and j are not quite the same in Kanarese as ch and j are in English or tsch and dsch in German; they are thinner, being produced by slightly pressing *the tip of the tongue only* to the gum of the upper front teeth.

ಞ ń *somewhat like* ny *in* Bunyan

This sound is produced with the same organs as the preceding four.

ಟ	ṭ	*cerebral* t
ಠ	ṭh	*the same aspirated*
ಡ	ḍ	*cerebral* d
ಢ	ḍh	*the same aspirated*
ಣ	ṇ	*cerebral* n

These five "*cerebral*" letters are produced by bending the tongue backwards and pressing the under side of its tip to the roof of the mouth.

ತ	t	*as* t *in the German* Ton *(without aspiration)*
ಥ	th	,, th ,, ,, ,, Thema, Rathaus *(strongly aspirated)*
ದ	d	,, d ,, ,, ,, leiden
ಧ	dh	,, d *aspirated* ,, standhaft
ನ	n	,, n *in* no ,, nirgends

These *dental* letters, being produced by pressing the tip of the tongue against the upper front teeth, differ from the corresponding English letters, which — at least the first four — are pronounced farther backwards approaching the cerebrals; also somewhat from the German dentals, which are produced at the gum.

ಪ p *as* p *in* pen *or* *German* Plage (*without aspiration*)

ಫ ph ,, ph ,, uphold *or* pin, ,, Pein (*strongly aspirated*)

This letter is not the Greek ph and should not be pronounced like f.

ಬ b *as* b *in* bold, *or German* gaben

ಭ bh ,, bh ,, abhor ,, habhaft

ಮ m ,, m ,, man ,, mann

ಯ y ,, y ,, yet *or* j *in* ,, ja

ರ r ,, r ,, ring, *or* ,, regen, schnurren

This letter should be pronounced with the tip of the tongue against the front teeth, and more trilled than the English r.

ಲ l *as* l *in* lie, *or German* liegen

Pronounced with the tip of the tongue against the front teeth.

ವ v *as the German* w *in* was

It is different from the English v as well as from w, being produced with the lips only, without the help of the teeth, and without rounding the lips as for w.

ಶ š *a peculiar soft* sh, produced by holding the tip of the tongue towards the upper gum and sounding s.

ಷ sh *as* sh *in* ship, the tongue is turned backwards as in pronouncing the cerebrals.

ಸ s *as* s *in* say, *German* sagen

ಹ h ,, h ,, hand, ,, Hand

ಳ ḷ *cerebral* l, produced with the same organs as the other cerebrals.

೦ This sign, as used in this book and in most Kanarese books, stands for any of the nasal sounds, ṅ, ń, ṇ, n, m, when standing before one of the gutterals, palatals, cerebrals, dentals or labials, and it takes

1. *the sound of* ṅ *that is* ng *before the* Gutterals k, kh, g, gh
2. *that* ,, ń ,, ,, ny ,, ,, Palatals č, čh, j, jh
3. ,, ,, ṇ ,, ,, Cerebrals ṭ, ṭh, ḍ, ḍh, ṇ
4. ,, ,, n ,, ,, Dentals t, th, d, dh, n
5. ,, ,, m ,, ,, Labials p, ph, b, bh, m

Besides this, it has a peculiar sound before y, r, l, v, s, h, etc.; but as these combinations do not occur in this book, we have nothing to do with them here.

2. A Vocabulary
of
162 Familiar Words in their simplest Form.

Nouns ನಾಮಗಳು.

Nouns in Kanarese are of three genders:—

(1) *Masculine* (m.) are the names of men, boys, and male deities;

(2) *Feminine* (f.) are the names of women, girls and goddesses;

(3) *Neuter* (n.) are the names of little children, sometimes of women in contempt, of animals, and of all lifeless beings and abstracts.

1.	ಕೈ	kei	hand
2.	ಕಾಲು	kâlu	foot
3.	ಬಾಯಿ	bâyi (bâi)	mouth
4.	ಕಣ್ಣು	kaṇṇu	eye
5.	ಕಿವಿ	kivi	ear
6.	ಅಪ್ಪ, ತಂದೆ	appa, tande	father
7.	ಅವ್ವ, ತಾಯಿ	avva, tâyi (tâi)	mother
8.	ಅಣ್ಣ	aṇṇa	elder brother
9.	ತಮ್ಮ	tamma	younger brother
10.	ಅಕ್ಕ	akka	elder sister
11.	ತಂಗಿ	taṅgi	younger sister
12.	ಮಗು	magu	child
13.	ಹೆಂಡತಿ	heṇḍati	wife
14.	ಹುಡುಗ, ಹುಡುಗಿ	huḍuga, huḍugi	boy, girl
15.	ಮಂದಿ	mandi	people, persons
16.	ಮಾತು	mâtu	word, saying, matter
17.	ಕೆಲಸ	kelasa	work, business
18.	ಮನೆ	mane	house
19.	ಬಾಗಲು, ಬಾಗಲ	bâgalu, bâgala	door
20.	ಊರು	ûru	town, village
21.	ಕತ್ತಿ	katti	knife, sword
22.	ಕೊಡೆ	koḍe	umbrella
23.	ಅಕ್ಕಿ	akki	rice (uncooked)

24. ಅನ್ನ	anna	boiled rice, food
25. ನೀರು	nîru	water
26. ಬೆಂಕಿ	benki	fire
27. ಊಟ	ûta	meal, dinner
28. ಎತ್ತು	*y*ettu	bullock, ox
29. ಕುದುರೆ	kudure	horse
30. ಗಾಡಿ	gâḍi	carriage
31. ಹೂ, ಹೂವು	hû, hûvu	flower
32. ದಿವಸ	divasa	a day
33. ರಾತ್ರಿ	râtri	night
34. ಹಗಲು	hagalu	daytime
35. ಹೊತ್ತು	hottu	sun, time
36. ಬಿಸಿಲು	bisilu	sunshine
37. ಘಂಟೆ	ghaṇṭe	bell, hour
38. ಗೊತ್ತು	gottu	certainty, knowledge
39. ಪಾಠ	pâṭha	lesson
40. ಕಷ್ಟ	kashṭa	pain, difficulty
41. ರೂಪಾಯಿ	rûpâyi	rupee

Pronouns ಸರ್ವನಾಮಗಳು.

42. ನಾ, ನಾನು	nâ, nânu	I
43. ನೀ, ನೀನು	nî, nînu	thou
44. ಇವ, ಈತ	iva, îta[1]	he *(if near)*
45. ಅವ, ಆತ	ava, âta[1]	he *(if far)*
46. ಇವಳು, ಈಕೆ	ivaḷu, îke[1]	she *(if near)*
47. ಅವಳು, ಆಕೆ	avaḷu, âke[1]	she *(if far)*
48. ಇದು	idu	this
49. ಅದು	adu	that
50. ತಾ, ತಾನು	tâ, tânu	self
51. ಯಾರು	yâru	who?
52. ಏನು	*y*ênu	what?

[1] The forms *îta, âta, îke, âke* are more polite than the other; they are extensively used in South-Mahratta, but seldom on the coast.

Adjectives ವಿಶೇಷಣಗಳು.

53. ಈ	î	this, these
54. ಆ	â	that, those
55. ಯಾವ	yâva	which? what?
56. ಇಷ್ಟು	ishṭu	this much, as many as these
57. ಅಷ್ಟು	ashṭu	that much, as many as those
58. ಎಷ್ಟು	*y*eshṭu	how much? how many?
59. ಇಂಥ, ಇಂಥಾ	intha, inthâ	such as this, . . . these
60. ಅಂಥ, ಅಂಥಾ	antha, anthâ	such as that. . . . those
61. ಎಂಥ, ಎಂಥಾ	*y*entha, *y*enthâ	what kind?
62. ಎಲ್ಲಾ	*y*ellâ	all
63. ಬಹಳ	bahaḷa	much, many
64. ಹೆಚ್ಚು	hečču	more
65. ತುಸ, ಸ್ವಲ್ಪ	tusa, svalpa	little, few
66. ಕೆಲವು	kelavu	some
67. ಒಳ್ಳೇ	*wo*ḷḷe	good
68. ಚಲೋ	čalô	nice, fine, good
69. ಹೊಸ	hosa	new
70. ಹಳೆ	haḷe	old
71. ದೊಡ್ಡ	doḍḍa	great, big
72. ಚಿಕ್ಕ, ಸಣ್ಣ	čikka, sanna	small, little

Verbs ಕ್ರಿಯಾಪದಗಳು.

73. ಇರು	iru	be
74. ಬಾ, ಬರು	bâ, baru	come
75. ತಾ, ತರು	tâ, taru	bring

---

1 We have given the verbs in their crude form, which in most cases, is the same as the 2nd person singular of the imperative mood; only in the verbs *bâ*, *tâ* crude forms *baru* and *taru* from which the other tenses are made, differ from the 2nd person singular imperative *bâ* and *tâ*.

76. ಆಗು	âgu	become, happen, be done
77. ಹೋಗು	hôgu	go
78. ಓದು	*w*ôdu	read
79. ಹಾಕು	hâku	throw, place
80. ತೋರು	tôru	appear, seem
81. ನೋಡು	nôḍu	look
82. ಮಾಡು	mâḍu	do, make
83. ಆಡು	âḍu	play
84. ಕಾಣು	kâṇu	see, appear
85. ಹೇಳು	hêḷu	say, tell
86. ಕೇಳು	kêḷu	hear, ask
87. ಏಳು	*y*êḷu	rise, get up
88. ಬೀಳು	bîḷu	fall
89. ಕೊಡು	koḍu	give
90. ಕೆಡು	keḍu	become bad, rot
91. ಬಿಡು	biḍu	leave, give up
92. ಇಡು	iḍu	put
93. ಅನ್ನು	annu	say
94. ತಿನ್ನು	tinnu	eat
95. ಉಣ್ಣು	uṇṇu	eat, (chiefly cooked food)
96. ನಿಲ್ಲು	nillu	stand
97. ಮುಚ್ಚು	mučču	shut
98. ಕೊಳ್ಳು	koḷḷu	take, buy
99. ಕೂಡ್ರು, ಕುಂಡ್ರು	kûḍru, kuṇḍru[1]	sit down
100. ಮಲಗು	malagu	lie down
101. ಬಾರಿಸು	bârisu	ring, play (an instrument)
102. ಕಳುಹಿಸು	kaḷuhisu	send
103. ಕರೆ	kare	call
104. ಬರಿ, ಬರೆ	bari, bare	write
105. ತೆಗಿ, ತೆಗೆ	tegi, tege	take away, remove

[1] The form *kuṇḍru* is considered vulgar by the educated classes.

Defective Verbs ಊನಕ್ರಿಯಾಪದಗಳು.

106. ಸಾಲು	sâlu	to be enough, to suffice
107. ಬೇಕು	bêku	is wanted, are wanted
108. ಬೇಡ	bêḍa	is not wanted, are not wanted
109. ಇಲ್ಲ	illa	is not, there is not, not
110. ಅಲ್ಲ	alla	is not so, not
111. ಉಂಟು	unṭu	is, are (*used in all genders and numbers*)
112. ಆರೆ, ಆರೆನು	âre, ârenu	I cannot

Adverbs ಕ್ರಿಯಾವಿಶೇಷಣಗಳು.

Most of them are originally nouns, capable of being declined and qualified by relative participles.

113. ಇನ್ನು	innu	yet, still, more
114. ದೂರ	dûra	far
115. ಇಲ್ಲಿ	illi	here
116. ಅಲ್ಲಿ	alli	there
117. ಎಲ್ಲಿ	*y*elli	where?
118. ಇಂದು	indu	to-day, now
119. ಅಂದು	andu	that day, then
120. ಎಂದು	*y*endu	when
121. ಈಗ	îga	now
122. ಆಗ	âga	then
123. ಯಾವಾಗ	yâvâga	when?
124. ಹೀಗೆ, ಹೀಂಗೆ	hîge, hînge	like this, thus, so
125. ಹಾಗೆ, ಹಾಂಗೆ	hâge, hânge[1]	like that, thus, so
126. ಹ್ಯಾಗೆ, ಹ್ಯಾಂಗೆ	hyâge, hyânge	how?
127. ಯಾಕೆ	yâke	why?
128. ಮಾತ್ರ	mâtra	only
129. ಹೌದು	houdu	yes
130. ಸೈ, ಸರಿ	sei, sari	right, well, good

[1] Also used as a postposition.

Prepositions ಉಪಸರ್ಗಗಳು.

In Kanarese they are placed after the genitive case of the word which they govern, and are therefore postpositions. Most of them are used as adverbs also.

They are, properly speaking, nouns, which, with the exception of Nos. 137 and 139, originally ended in *u*, or a consonant, as *mundu*, *hindu*, *mêl*, *kelagu* etc. The termination *e* is a kind of locative termination, expressing "in" or "on"; so that the proper meaning of *munde* is=in the front part, *mêle*=in the upper part, on the upper side, in after time, etc. By keeping this in mind, their construction in sentences will be easily understood.

131. ಮುಂದೆ	munde	before, in front
132. ಹಿಂದೆ	hinde	behind, after
133. ಮೇಲೆ	mêle	on, after
134. ಕೆಳಗೆ	keḷage	below
135. ಒಳಗೆ	*wo*ḷage	within, in
136. ಹೊರಗೆ	horage	without, out
137. ಹತ್ತರ	hattara	near
138. ಮುಂಚೆ	muñče	before
139. ತನಕ	tanaka	till, as far as

Affixes ನಿಪಾತಗಳು.

140. ಏ	ê	even, just (*emphatic affix*)[1]
141. ಓ, ಆ	ô, â	(*interrogative affix*)[2]
142. ಊ	û	also, too, even (*copulation affix*)
143. ರೆ	re	if (*affix of condition*)
144. ಇಂತ	inta	than (*affix of comparison*)

[1] In the following phrases and sentences it is generally not translated at all, but marked with Italics.

[2] Generally rendered only by a sign of interrogation (?) after the word to which it is affixed.

Numeral Adjectives ಸಂಖ್ಯಾವಾಚಕಗಳು.

145.	ಒಂದು, ಒಬ್ಬ	*wondu* (*n.*), *wobba* (*m. & f.*)[1]	one
146.	ಎರಡು, ಇಬ್ಬರು	*yeraḍu* (*n.*), ibbaru (*m. & f.*)[2]	two
147.	ಮೂರು, ಮೂವರು	mûru (*n.*), mûvaru (*m. & f.*)	three
148.	ನಾಲ್ಕು, ನಾಲ್ವರು	nâlku (*n.*), nâlvaru (*m. & f.*)	four
149.	ಐದು, ಐವರು	eidu (*n.*), eivaru (*m. & f.*)	five
150.	ಆರು	âru (*n.*)	six
151.	ಏಳು	*yêḷu* (*n.*)	seven
152.	ಎಂಟು	*yeṇṭu* (*n.*)	eight
153.	ಒಂಭತ್ತು	*wombhattu* (*n.*)	nine
154.	ಹತ್ತು	hattu (*n.*)	ten
155.	ಹನ್ನೊಂದು	hannondu (*n.*)	eleven
156.	ಹನ್ನೆರಡು	hanneradu (*n.*)	twelve
157.	ಹದಿಮೂರು	hadimûru (*n.*)	thirteen
158.	ಹದಿನಾಲ್ಕು	hadinâlku (*n.*)	fourteen
159.	ಹದಿನೈದು	hadineidu (*n.*)	fifteen
	etc.	etc.	etc.
160.	ಹತ್ತೊಂಭತ್ತು	hattombhattu (*n.*)	nineteen
161.	ಇಪ್ಪತ್ತು	ippattu (*n.*)	twenty
162.	ನೂರು	nûru (*n.*)	a hundred

---

[1] *wobba* derived from *worva*=*wor* (one)+va (the personal affix).

[2] ibbaru, from irvaru=ir (two)+varu (the personal affix in the plural).

3. One Thousand Phrases and Sentences composed of the Words of the Vocabulary

1. ಬರು **baru**=to come; ಹೋಗು **hôgu**=to go (*G. Kommen, gehen*).

Conjugation of Verbs ending in u.

Present verbal participle:	**bar-utta**=coming (never used as an adjective).
Present and future relative participle:	**bar-uva**=coming, (he) who comes or is coming, (that) which comes (*used as an adjective*)
Infinitive:	**bar-a, bar-alu, bar-alikke**=to come
Verbal noun:	**bar-uvadu**=the coming

Present Tense.

Singular:	*Plural:*
barutt-êne, I come, am coming	**barutt-êve,** we come, are coming
barutt-î, thou comest, art coming	**barutt-îri,** you ,, ,,
barutt-âne, he comes, is coming	**barutt-âre,** they (*mas. & fem.*) come, are coming
barutt-âḷe, she comes, is coming	
barutt-ade, it comes, is coming	**barutt-ave,** they (*neut.*) come, are coming

Imperative singular: **bâ,** come;	**barali,** let me (him, her, it) come
,, *Plural:* **barri or banni** come;	**barali,** let them come
Imperative singular: **hôgu,** go;	**hôgali,** let me (him, her, it) go
,, *Plural:* **hôgiri,** go;	**hôgali,** let them go

Remarks: In the same manner all the verbs on pp. 6 and 7, except those ending in o or i, are conjugated.

ಇಲ್ಲಿ ಬಾ	**illi bâ**
Come here	here come
ಬರುತ್ತೇನೆ	**baruttêne**
I am coming	I come
ಯಾರು ಬರುತ್ತಾರೆ?	**yâru baruttâre?**
Who is coming? who will come?	who they come?

ನಾನು ಬರುತ್ತೇನೆ	**nânu baruttêne**
I am coming, I shall come	I I come
ಒಬ್ಬ ಹುಡುಗ ಬರುತ್ತಾನೆ	***w*obba huḍuga baruttâne**
A boy is coming, will come	one boy he comes
ಅವ್ವ ಬರುತ್ತಾಳೆ	**avva baruttâḷe**
My mother is coming	mother she comes
ಒಂದು ಕುದುರೆ ಬರುತ್ತದೆ	***w*ondu kudure baruttade**
A horse is coming, will come	one horse it comes
ಯಾವಾಗ ಹೋಗುತ್ತೀರಿ?	**yâvâga hôguttîri?**
When are you going?	when you go
ನಾಳೆ ಹೋಗುತ್ತೇವೆ	**nâḷe hôguttêve**
We shall go to-morrow	to-morrow we go
ನಾವು ಹೋಗುವದಿಲ್ಲ	**nâvu hôguvad' illa**[1]
We are not going, we shall not go	we the going is not

2. ಬರು baru, ಹೋಗು hôgu (*continued*).

Past verbal part.—**bandu** = being come; **hôgi** = having gone

Past relat. part.—**banda** = (he) who is come; (that) which is come; **hôda** = (he) who is gone, (that) which is gone

Past verbal noun.—**bandaddu** = 1. the having come; 2. the thing come. **hôdaddu** = 1. the being (or having) gone; 2. the thing gone.

---

[1] *Hôguvad' illa* = *hoguvadu-illa*.—When the final *a* or *u* and sometimes *i* of a word is followed by the initial vowel of another word, or of a termination, it is generally dropped, and the two words are spoken as one word. Sometimes this euphonic union (Kan. *sandhi*) takes place even before a consonant. In future this kind of elision will always be marked with an apostrophe.

The verbal noun in Kanarese differs from that in English and German by retaining its verbal capacity of taking a subject, whereas in English the agent must be added in the form of a possessive case or a possessive pronoun, *e. g.* nâvu hôguvadu = our going; avaru hôguvadu = their going; kudure hôguvadu = the horse's going; avanu bandaddu (see No. 2) = his having come. Objects and adverbs also may be added to the Kanarese verbal noun.

Past Tense.

Singular:	*Plural:*
band-e(nu), I came	**band-evu,** we came
band-i, thou camest	**band-iri,** you came
band-a(nu), he came. **band-a(ḷu),** she came	**band-aru,** they (*m. & f.*) came
ban-tu, it came	**band-avu,** they (*n.*) came
hôd-e(nu), I went	**hôd-evu,** we went
hôd-i, etc. (*just like* bandenu)	etc.
hôyitu, it went	

Remarks:—The past tense is formed by adding the termination *enu, i, anu, aḷu, itu, evu, iri, aru, avu* to the past relative participle, whose last vowel *a* is dropped; as' banda+enu=bandenu; hôda+iri=hôdiri; mâḍida (*the past rel. part. of* mâḍu) mâḍidenu; only tho formation of the 3rd person, neuter, of the singular number is irregular. Colloquially the termination *nu* is often omitted.

ಯಾವಾಗ ಬಂದ?	**yâvâga banda?**
When did he come?	when he came
ನಿನ್ನೆ ಬಂದು ಹೋದ	**ninne bandu hôda**
He came yesterday and went away [again	yesterday h.[1] come he went
ಬಂದದ್ದು ಚಲೋದು[2]	**bandaddu[2] čalôdu**
It is well that he came (is come)	the h. come good
ಹೋಗಿ ಬರ್ರಿ (ಬನ್ನಿ)	**hôgi barri (banni)**
Go and come back	h.[1] gone come
ಹೋಗಿ ಬರುತ್ತೇನೆ	**hôgi baruttêne**
I am going[3]	h.[1] gone I come
ನಾ(ನು) ಹೋಗುವದಿಲ್ಲ	**nâ(nu) hôguvad'illa**
I am not going, I shall not go	my going[4] is not
ನೀ ಯಾಕೆ ಹೋಗುವದಿಲ್ಲ?	**nî yâke hôguvad'illa?**
Why are you not going?	Why thy going[4] is not

---

[1] H. come=having come; for the sake of brevity the English for the past verbal participle will in future always be abbreviated thus.

[2] Čalôdu=čalô+du; see Remark 2, page 18.

[3] Though the literal meaning of this sentence is "I am going, but shall return", yet it is generally used in leave taking.

[4] See note 1 page 12. Though the phrase literally means: "I the going", it will, when possible, for the sake of brevity and convenience in future be translated: "my

ನಾ ಯಾಕೆ ಹೋಗಲಿ?	nâ yâke hôgali?
Why should I go?	I why let (me) go
ಅವನು ಬಂದ ಮೇಲೆ ಹೋಗುತ್ತೇನೆ	avanu banda mêle[1] hôguttêne
I shall go after his arrival	he coming after I go
ಹೌದು, ಹೋಗಬೇಕು	houdu, hôga bêku
Yes, you must go	yes, to go is wanted

3. ಅನ್ನು **annu** = to say (*G. sagen*);
ಅಂದು **andu** = having said; ಅಂದಿತು **anditu** = it said.
(Conjugated like *baru.*)

ಏನಂದಿ?	*y*ên andi?
What did you say?	what thou saidst
ಬಾ ಅಂದೆ	bâ ande
I told you to come	come I said
ಏನೂ ಅನ್ನಲಿಲ್ಲ	*y*ênû annal'illa[2]
I (*a. p.*)[3] did not say anything	what even to say not
ಹ್ಯಾಗನ್ನ ಬೇಕು?	hyâg'anna bêku?
How should I (*a. p.*) say?	how to say is wanted

going"; *nînu hôguvadu* will be translated: "thy going", etc. The present verbal noun, combined with *illa*, is used to form a kind of negative present tense; as, *nânu hôguvad'illa*, I do not go, am not going; *nînu hôguvad'illa*, thou dost not go, art not going; *avanu hôguvad'illa*, he does not go, is not going, etc.

[1] *Banda mêle,*—to understand this and similar phrases, it should be remembered (see p. 9, Remark to the Prepositions), that *mêle* is, properly speaking, a noun with a locative termination, meaning "in after time"; the literal meaning of *avanu banda mêle* is therefore, "in the aftertime (following that in) which he came", *i. e.* after his coming. It should further be noted that the Kanarese relative participle permits of a more unlimited application than English participles; *e. g. banda divasa*, the day which is come; but *avanu banda divasa*, the day on which he came; *nîvu banda divasa*, the day on which you came; *nâvu baruva divasa*, the day on which we shall come, etc.

[2] See note 1 p. 12. The second form of the infinitive mood (as, *annalu, baralu, hôgalu*) is much used to form a kind of negative past tense, as *nânu annal'illa*, I did not say; *nînu annal'illa* thou didst not say; *avanu annal'illa*, he did not say, etc.

[3] The letters *a. p.* in parenthesis, meaning *any person*, are used to show that the verb impersonal and may be used equally with the 1st, 2nd, or 3rd person.

ಹೀಗನ್ನ ಬೇಕು	**hîg' anna bêku**
You *(a. p.)* should say thus	thus to say is wanted
ಅವನು ಅಂದ ಮಾತೇನು?	**avanu anda mât'ênu?**
What did he say?	he which (he) said word what
ನೀನಂದದ್ದೇನು?	**nîn' andadd' ênu?**
What did you say?	thou which saidst what
ಇದಕ್ಕೇನನ್ನುತ್ತಾರೆ?[1] [this called?	**idakk'[1] ên' annuttâre?**
What do they say to it? or what is	to this what they say
ಬರುತ್ತಾರಂತೆ[2]	**baruttâr' ante[2]**
They are coming, I am told	they come it says
ಬಂದರಂತೆ	**bandar' ante**
They are come, I am told	they come it says

4. ಅವ ava = he, that man, ಇವ **iva** = he, this man, ಆತ âṭa = he; ಈತ îta = he *(hon.)* (*G. er, jener, dieser*).

Declension of Masculine Nouns and Pronouns ending in ಅ a

	Singular:	*Plural:*
1. *Nominative,*	**ava-n-u**, he	**ava-r-u**, they
2. *Accusative,*	**ava-n-annu**, him	**ava-r-annu**, them
3. *Instrumental,*	**ava-n-inda**, by him, from him	**ava-r-inda**, by them, from them
4. *Dative,*	**ava-n-ige**, to him	**ava-r-ige**, to them
5. *Ablative,*	**ava-n-a-deseyinda** for him, on his account	**ava-r-a-deseyinda**, for them, on their account
6. *Genitive,*	**ava-n-a**, his	**ava-r-a**, their
7. *Locative,*	**ava-n-alli**, in him, on him	**ava-r-alli**, in them, on them

Remarks: 1. Each case consists of the crude form (here *ava*), a connecting sound (here *n* in the singular, and *r* in the plural), and the termination. The terminations are the same (the Dative excepted) for all declensions and for singular and plural. The connective letter only is changed. It is ḷ for the feminine gender, as, *avaḷu* = she, *avaḷannu*, *avaḷinda*, etc.

---

[1] About the form *idakke* see *idu* p. 18.

[2] *Ante*, derived from *annuttade* = it says, is added at the end of a sentence to express that the sentence is the saying of some other person, or of rumour; compare the French „on dit".

2. *Iva, âta, îta* are declined in the same way; also the numeral adjective wobba; whereas *ibbaru, mûvaru, nâlvaru, eivaru* follow the plural *avaru.*

3. The ablative is, properly speaking, not a particular case, but it is the genitive followed by the instrumental of the word *dese,* it will therefore be omitted in future.

ಎಲ್ಲಿಯ **yelliya**=of what place,

ಧಾರವಾಡದ **dhâravâḍada**=of Dharwar   ಊರಿನ **ûrina**=of the town,

ಮಂಗಳೂರಿನ **mangaḷûrina**=of Mangalore.

ಅವನು ಯಾರು?	**avanu yâru?**
Who is he?	he who
ಅವನ ಹೆಸರೇನು?	**avana hesar' ênu?**
What is his name?	his name what
ಅವನು ಯಾವ ಊರಿನವ?	**avanu yâva ûrin ava?**[1]
Of what place is he?	he what of town he
ಈತನು ಧಾರವಾಡದವ[1]	**îtanu dhâravâḍad' ava**[1]
This is a Dharwar man	this man of Dharwar he
ಆತನು ಮಂಗಳೂರಿನವ[1]	**âtanu mangaḷûrin' ava**[1]
That is a Mangalore man	that man of Mangalore he
ಈಗ ಬಂದವರ್ಯಾರು?	**îga band' avar' yâru?**
Who are the persons just come?	now who came they who
ಅವರು ದೊಡ್ಡವರು	**avaru doḍḍ'avaru**[2]
They are big men, rich men	they great ones
ಅವರನ್ನು ಕರೆ	**avarannu kare**
Call them	them call
ಅವರಿಗೆ ನೀರು ಕೊಡು	**avarige nîru**[3] **koḍu**
Give them some water	to them water give
ಆ ಚಿಕ್ಕವನಿಗೆ ಹೂ ಕೊಡಿರಿ	**â čikk'avanige hû**[3] **koḍiri**
Give that little one some flowers	that to little one flower give

---

[1] The crude form, instead of the nominative, is generally used colloquially.

[2] Doḍḍ'avaru, čikk'avanu; these and similar compounds will in future in the interlinear translation be rendered: — great ones, little ones, and the like. Further particulars about these compounds see No. 28.

[3] The crude form is often used instead of the accusative case when it can be done without causing ambiguity.

5. ಮಾತು **mâtu**=word, saying, matter (*G. Wort, Sache*).

Declension of Nouns ending in a movable ಉ u.

	Singular:	*Plural:*
1. *Nominative,*	**mâtu,** the word or a word	**mâtu-gaḷ-u,** the words
2. *Accusative,*	**mât-annu,** the word	**mâtu-gaḷ-annu,** the words
3. *Instrumental,*	**mât-in-inda,** by, from or with the word	**mâtu-gaḷ-inda,** by, from or with the words
4. *Dative,*	**mât-ige,** to the w.	**mâtu-gaḷ-ige,** to the words
6. *Genitive,*	**mât-in-a,** of the w.	**mâtu-gaḷ-a,** of the words
7. *Locative,*	**mât-in-alli,** in or on the word	**mâtu-gaḷ-alli,** in or on the words

Remark.—All the nouns terminating in *u*, on pp. 4 and 5 of the Vocabulary, except *magu* are declined in the same way.

ಯಾವ ಮಾತು ಹೇಳಿದ?	**yâva mâtu[1] hêḷida?**
What did he say? What word did he use?	what word he said
ಈ ಮಾತು ಹೇಳ ಬೇಡ	**î mâtu[1] hêḷa bêḍa**
Do not say this; Do not tell this matter	this word to say is not wanted
ಈ ಮಾತುಗಳು ಒಳ್ಳೇ ಮಾತುಗಳಲ್ಲ	**î mâtugaḷu** ***woḷḷê*** **mâtugaḷ' alla**
These are improper words	these words good words not
ನೀನು ಮಾತು ಕೇಳುವದಿಲ್ಲ	**nînu mâtu[1] kêḷuvad' illa**
You are disobedient	thou word the hearing is not
ಈ ಮಾತಿಗೇನು ಹೇಳಲಿ?	**î mâtig' ênu hêḷali?**
What can I say to this? . . . this [matter?	this to the word what let me tell
ಏನು ಮಾತಾಡುತ್ತೀರಿ?	***y*****ênu mât' âḍuttîri?**
What are you talking about?	what word you play
ಇದು ದೊಡ್ಡ ಮಾತಲ್ಲ	**idu doḍḍa mât' alla**
It is not a great matter	the great word not
ಈ ಮಾತಿನಲ್ಲಿ ಏನೂ ಇಲ್ಲ	**î mâtinalli** ***y*****ên'û illa**
There is nothing in the matter	this in the word what even is not

[1] *Mâtu,* the crude form instead of the accusative *mâtannu,* see note 3 p. 16.

ಮಾತು ಕೊಡುತ್ತೇನೆ — **mâtu koḍuttêne**
I give my word; I promise — word I give

ಅವರ ಮಾತಿನ ಮೇಲೆ ಬರುತ್ತೇನೆ — **avara mâtina mêle baruttêne**
I shall come relying on their (his) promise — their of the word on I come

6. ಅದು **adu**=that; ಇದು **idu**=this; Pronouns (*G. jenes, dieses*).
ಆ **â**=that, those; ಈ **î**=this, these; Adjectives
(*G. jener, jene, jenes; dieser, diese, dieses*).
Irregular Declension of **a d u**.

	Singular:	*Plural:*
1. Nom.	**adu**, that, it	**avu, avu-gaḷ-u**, those (*i. e.* those things), they
2. Acc.	**ad-annu**, that	**av-annu, avu-gaḷ-annu**, those (things), them
3. Instr.	**ad-ar-inda**, by, from, or with that	**avu-gaḷ-inda**, by, from, with those (things)
4. Dat.	**ad-akke**, to that	**av-akke, avu-gaḷ-ige**, to those (things)
6. Gen.	**ad-ar-a**, of that	**avu-gaḷ-a**, of those (things)
7. Loc.	**ad-ar-alli**, in that	**avu-gaḷ-alli**, in those (things)

Remarks:—1. *Idu* and all the neuter numeral adjectives on p. 10 follow *adu* in their declension, as do also the verbal nouns, such as **b a r u v a d u, b a n d a d d u.**

2. Adjectives, relative participles, and genitive cases of nouns and pronouns get, the force of nouns or pronouns by having the syllable *du* (instead of *adu*) added to them, and are then capable of being declined like *adu;* for instance:— **d o ḍ ḍ a**=great, **d o ḍ ḍ a d u**, a great one, a great thing; **h ô d a**=which is gone, **h ô d a d d u**=that which is gone; **n a n n a**=my, **n a n n a d u**=mine; **n a m m a**=our, **n a m m a d u**=ours, etc. When added to past relative participles, the *d* of *du* is generally doubled, as **b a n d a d d u** for **b a n d a d u**,

ಅದೇನು? — **ad ênu?**
What is that? — that what

ಅದು ಒಂದು ಮನೆ — **adu wondu mane**
That is a house — that one house

ಆ ಮನೆ ಯಾರದು? — **â mane yâradu**[1]**?**
Whose house is that? — that house whose

---

[1] See Remark 2 above.

ಅದು ನನ್ನದು	**adu nannadu**[1]
It is mine	that mine
ಈ ಮನೆ ಹಳೇದು	**î mane haḷêdu**[1]
This house is old	this house an old one
ಅದು ಹೊಸದು	**adu hosadu**[1]
That is new	that a new one
ಅದನ್ನು ಕೊಡುತ್ತಾರೆ	**adannu koḍuttâre**
They give that; or that is to be sold	that they give
ಅದಕ್ಕೇನು ಕೊಡುತ್ತೀ?	**adakk' ênu koḍuttî?**
What will you give for it?	to that what thou givest
ಈ ಕುದುರೆಗಳು ಯಾರವು?	**î kuduregaḷu**[2] **yâravu?**
Whose horse are these?	these horses whose
ಇವು ನಮ್ಮವು	**ivu nammavu**
They are ours	these ours

7. ನಾ **nâ**, ನಾನು **nânu** = I (*G. ich*); ನೀ **nî**, ನೀನು **nînu** = thou (*G. du*).

Irregular declension of the First and Second Personal Pronouns.

	Singular:	*Plural:*
1. *Nom.*	**nânu**, I	**nâvu**, we
2. *Acc.*	**nannannu**, me	**nammannu**, us
3. *Instr.*	**nanninda**, by or from me	**namminda**, by or from us
4. *Dat.*	**nanage**, to me	**namage**, to us
6. *Gen.*	**nanna**, my	**namma**, our
7. *Loc.*	**nannalli**, in or on me	**nammalli**, in or on us

Remarks:—1. **Nînu** and **tânu** are declined in the same way as **nânu**.

2. **Nânu** with the emphatic affix ê = **nânê**, signifies myself; **nînê**, thyself; **tânê**, himself.

ನೀನಿರು, ನಾ ಹೋಗುತ್ತೇನೆ	**nîn' iru, nâ hôguttêne**
You stay, I shall go	thou be, I go
ಈ ಕೆಲಸ ನಾನೇ ನೋಡುತ್ತೇನೆ	**î kelasa nânê nôḍuttêne**
I shall see to this business myself	this business myself I look

[1] See Remark 2 on p. 18.

[2] *Kuduregaḷu* is plural of *kudure*, see Declension of nouns ending in *e*, No. 20.

ಇದು ನನ್ನ ಕೆಲಸ	**idu nanna kelasa**
This is my business (work)	this my business
ನನ್ನನ್ನು ನೋಡಿರಿ	**nannannu nôḍiri**
Look at me	me look
ನನ್ನಿಂದಾಗುವದಿಲ್ಲ	**nannind' âguvad illa**[1]
I cannot do it	by me the being done is not
ನನಗೆ ಕೇಳುತ್ತಾರೆ	**nanage kêḷuttâre**
They will ask me; it will be asked of me	to me they ask
ನನಗೆ ಒಂದು ರೂಪಾಯಿ ಕೊಡು	**nanage *w*ondu rûpâyi koḍu**
Give me one rupee	to me one rupee give
ನನ್ನಲ್ಲಿ ಏನೂ ಇಲ್ಲ	**nannalli *y*ên'û illa**
I have nothing (no money) with me	in me what even is not
ಇದು ಯಾರದು? ಇದು ನನ್ನದು	**idu yâradu? idu nannadu**
Whose is this? It is mine	this whose? this mine
ನಾನೇ ಮಾಡಿದೆ	**nânê mâḍide**
I made it myself	myself I made

8. *The same continued.*

ನಾನಿರುತ್ತೇನೆ, ನೀ ಹೋಗು	**nân'iruttêne, ni hôgu**
You go, and I shall stay	I am, thou go
ಈ ಕೆಲಸ ನೀನೇ ಮಾಡಿದಿ	**î kelasa nînê mâḍidi**
It is you who has done this	this business thyself thou didst
ನೀನು ಬರುತ್ತೀಯೋ, ಅವನು ಬರುತ್ತಾನೋ?	**nînu baruttîyô, avanu baruttân'ô**[2]**?**
Will you come, or he?	thou comest, he comes?
ಇದು ನಿನ್ನ ಮಾತು	**idu ninna mâtu**
This is your concern	this thy matter
ಇದು ನಿನ್ನದೇನು? (*S.*) ನಿನ್ನದೋ? (*C.*)[3]	**idu ninnad' ênu? ninnad'ô?**
Is this yours?	this thine what? thine?

---

[1] See note 4 p. 13.

[2] When a vowel is immediately followed by another vowel, the first is either omitted, as in *baruttân'ô* (= *baruttâne* + *ô*), or one of the consonants *v* and *y* is inserted, between; *v* is inserted after an *a* or *u*, and *y* after *e* or *i*; as, *baruttî* + *ô* = *baruttîyô?*

[3] In the Southern Maharatta districts (*S.*) *ênu*, in Kanara (*C.*), and Mysore *ô* is added after a word or sentence to give it an interrogative force.

ನಿನ್ನನ್ನು ಬಿಡುವದಿಲ್ಲ	**ninnannu biḍuvad' illa**
I (*a.p.*) shall not leave you alone	thee the leaving is not
ನಿಮ್ಮಿಂದಾಗುವದೋ?	**nimmind' âguvad'ô?**
Can you do it?	by you the being done?
ನಮ್ಮಿಂದಾಗುವದಿಲ್ಲ	**nammind' âguvad' illa**
We cannot do it; it is impossible for us	by us the being done is not
ನಿನ್ನಲ್ಲಿ ಕೆಟ್ಟದ್ದೇನೂ ಕಾಣುವದಿಲ್ಲ	**ninnalli keṭṭadd'ên'û[1] kâṇuvad' [illa**
I can't see any wrong in you	in thee bad what even the appearing is not
ನಿಮ್ಮ ದೆಸೆಯಿಂದ ಬಂದೆ	**nimma deseyinda bande**
I am come on your account	on your account I come

9. ಎಲ್ಲಾ **yellâ** = all, everything (*G. alles*).

Irregular Declension.

	Singular:		*Plural:*
1. Nom.	**yellâ**, all, everything	*Masc. & fem.*	**yellaru**, all, persons, *declined like* avaru
2. Acc.	**yellavannu, yellânnu**, all		
3. Instr.	**yellâdarinda**, from, by, or with all	*Neut.*	**yellavu, yellavugaḷu**, all things, *declined like* avu, avugaḷu
4. Dat.	**yellâdakke**, to all		
6. Gen.	**yellâdara**, of all		
7. Loc.	**yellâdaralli**, in all		

Remarks:—1. When standing before the noun which it qualifies, *yellâ* is not declined.

2. When following the noun it qualifies, *yellâ* is either attached to the crude form (in neuter nouns) or the nominative case plural; in these two cases it is declined as above; or it is attached to the different cases of nouns, when itself is not declined.

ಎಲ್ಲಾ ಹೋಯಿತು	**yellâ hôyitu**
Everything is gone; all gone	all it went
ಎಲ್ಲರೂ ಹೋದರು	**yellar'û hôdaru**
Every one went; .... is gone	all even went

[1] *Keṭṭaddu* is the verbal noun, past tense of *kêḍu*, signifying (1) the action of having grown bad, (2) that which has grown bad, something bad wicked or corrupt; *yênû*=*yênu*+*û*, what even, followed by *illa*, means, there is nothing.

ನೀ ಕರದವರೆಲ್ಲರೂ ಬಂದಿರುತ್ತಾರೆ	**nî karad' avar' ellar'û**[1] **band' iruttâre**
All those whom you called are come	you whom you called they all even h. come they are
ಎಲ್ಲರ ಹಿಂದೆ ನಾನು ಬಂದೆ	**yellara hinde nânu bande**
I came last of all	of all behind I came
ಎಲ್ಲಾ ಆದ ಮೇಲೆ ಹೋದೆ	**yellâ âda**[2] **mêle hôde**
I went away when all was over	all after happening I went
ಎಲ್ಲಾ ನಿನ್ನದು	**yellâ ninnadu**
All is yours	all thine
ನನ್ನದೆಲ್ಲಾ ನಿನ್ನದೇ	**nannad'ellâ ninnadê**
All that is mine is yours	mine all thine
ಇವನು ಎಲ್ಲರಲ್ಲಿ ದೊಡ್ಡವನು	**ivanu yellaralli doḍḍavanu**
He is the eldest of all	he in all a great one
ಇದು ಎಲ್ಲವುಗಳಲ್ಲಿ ಚಲೋದು	**idu yellavugaḷalli čalôdu**
This is the nicest of all	this in all (things) a nice one
ಅವರೆಲ್ಲರನ್ನು ಕರೆ	**avar' ellarannu kare**
Call them all	them all call

10. ಆಗು âgu = to become, to be done, to be finished, to happen (*G. werden, geschehen*).

Present and past tenses are conjugated like h ô g u.

1st Future Tense.

Singular:	*Plural:*
âd-ênu, I shall (probably) become	**âd-êvu,** we shall (probably) become
âd-î, thou wilt ,, ,,	**âd-îri,** you will ,, ,,
âd-ânu, he will ,, ,,	**âd-âru,** they (*m. & f.*) will ,, ,,
âd-âḷu, she will ,, ,,	
âd-îtu, it will ,, ,,	**âd-âvu,** they (*n.*) will ,, ,,

Remarks:—The affixes ê n u, î, â n u, etc. are added to the past relative participle whose final *a* is dropped; as, â d a + ê n u = â d ê n u. In those verbs on *u*, whose past relative participle ends in *ida* the syllable *da* is dropped; as m â ḍ u, past relative participle m â ḍ i d a + ê n u = m â ḍ i + ê n u = m â ḍ y ê n u; frequently the whole termination *i d a* is omitted; as, m â ḍ ê n u.

---

1 *Karada* is past relative participle of *kare,* see No. 18.

2 The same form as *hôda* in No. 2.

ಆಯಿತು	**âyitu**
It is done; it is finished	it became, it was done
ಆದೀತು	**âdîtu**
It may happen; it will do	it may be done
ಆಗುವದಿಲ್ಲ	**âguvad' illa**
It is not done; it's impossible	the becoming is not
ಒಳ್ಳೆಯವನಾದನು	***w*****oḷḷe-y-avan' âdanu**
He became a good man (boy)	a good one he became
ಹಳೇದಾಯಿತು	**haḷêd' âyitu**
It has grown old	an old one it became
ಏಳು ಘಂಟೆ ಆಯಿತು	***y*****êḷu ghaṇṭe âyitu**
It is seven o'clock	seven bell it became
ರಾತ್ರಿಯಾಯಿತು	**râtri-y-âyitu**[1]
The night has set in; it's night	night it became
ದೊಡ್ಡದಾಗುತ್ತದೆ	**doḍḍad' âguttade**
It will become greater; it is growing	a great one it becomes
ಬಹಳ ಆಗಲಿಲ್ಲ	**bahaḷa âgal' illa**[2]
It is not much; they are not many	much to become is not
ರಾತ್ರಿಯಾದ ಮೇಲೆ	**râtri-y-âda mêle**[3]
After nightfall	night after becoming

11. ಇರು iru = to be (G. *sein*)

The Present Tense is conjugated like baru.

Remarks:—Instead of the verb iruttêne, the compound verb iddhêne, iddhî, iddhâne, iddhâḷe, iddhe, iddhêve, iddhîri, iddhâre, iddhâve, ive or ave, or iddêne, iddî, iddâne, etc. is much used in some districts, chiefly on the coast; it is composed of the past verbal participle iddu (=irdu, derived from iru)=having been, and hêne, hî, hâne, etc.=I am; this latter form is still in use in some eastern districts. Colloquially the forms adêne, adî, adâne, adâḷe, ade, adêve, etc. are common in the Southern Maharatta districts.

The past tense is formed of the past verbal participle iddu; as iddenu iddi, etc., 3rd person neuter ittu; past relative participle idda.

---

[1] See note 1 p. 25.

[2] See note 2 p. 14.

[3] See note 1 p. 14.

ಎಲ್ಲಿರುತ್ತೀರಿ?	*y*ell' iruttîri
Where are you? where do you live?	where you are
ಈ ಮನೆಯಲ್ಲಿರುತ್ತೇನೆ	î maneyall' iruttêne[1]
I live in this house	this in house I am
ರಾತ್ರಿಯಲ್ಲಿ ಎಲ್ಲಿದ್ದಿ?	râtriyalli *y*ell' iddi?
Where have you been during the night?	in the night where thou wast
ಮನೆಯಲ್ಲಿದ್ದೆ	maneyall' idde
I was at home	in the house I was
ಅವನು ಊರಿಗೆ ಹೋಗಿದ್ದ	avanu ûrige hôg' idda[2]
He had gone into the country (with some stress on "he")	he to town h. gone he was
ಊರಿಗೆ ಹೋಗಿದ್ದ	ûrige hôg idda
He had gone into the country (without stress on "he")	to town h. gone he was
ನಾನಿರುವ ಮನೆ ದೊಡ್ಡದು	nân' iruva[3] mane doḍḍadu
The house I live in is a large one	I being house a large one
ನೀವಿರುವದು ಎಲ್ಲಿ?	nîv' iruvadu[4] *y*elli?
Where do you live?	your being where
ಅವರಿರುತ್ತಾರೋ? *C.* ಅವರಿರುತ್ತಾರೇನು? *S.*	avar' iruttârô? *C.* avar' iruttâr' ênu? *S.*
Are they (is he) here ?—at home?	they are they? they are what
ಇರುವದಿಲ್ಲ *or* ಇಲ್ಲ	iruvad'[4] illa, *or* illa
They (*a. p.*) are not here; no	the being is not, is not

12. ಇರು iru (*continued*).

ಎಷ್ಟು ದಿವಸ ಇರುತ್ತೀರಿ?	*y*eshṭu divasa iruttîri?
How long will you stay?	how many day you are
ಒಂದೇ ದಿವಸ ಇರುತ್ತೇವೆ	*w*ondê divasa iruttêve
We shall stay only one day	*one* day we are

---

1 *Maneyalli* is the locative case of *mane*, *râtriyalli* of *râtri;* see declension of nouns ending in *e* and *i*, No. 20.

2 *Hôgi*+*idda;* the past verbal participle (*hôgi*), combined with the past tense of *iru*, forms the pluperfect tense; as *hôgi*+*iddenu*=*hôgiddenu*, I had gone. Colloquially the termination *nu* is omitted.

3 Present relative participle; *iruva mane* signifies the house which is, but *nânu iruva mane*, the house in which I am; *nîvu iruva mane*, the house in which you are, etc. See note 1 p. 14.

4 See note 1 p. 12.

ಎಲ್ಲಿ ಅದೆ (ಉಂಟು *C.*)?	**yelli ade (uṇṭu** *C.*)?
Where is it?	where it is (it is, *a. p.*)
ಇಲ್ಲಿ ಅದೆ (ಉಂಟು *C.*)	**illi ade (uṇṭu** *C.*)
It is here	here it is (it is, *a. p.*)
ಈ ಕೊಡೆ ಎಲ್ಲಿ ಇತ್ತು?	**î koḍe yelli ittu?**
Where was this umbrella?	this umbrella where it was
ಮನೆಯಲ್ಲಿ ಇದ್ದಿಲ್ಲ (ಇರಲಿಲ್ಲ *C.*)	**maneyalli idd' illa (iral'illa** *C.*)[1]
It was not in the house	in the house h. been is not (to be not)
ಇದ್ದವರೆಲ್ಲರೂ ಬರಲಿ	**idd' avar'ellar'û barali**
Let them all come	who were they all even let them come
ಇದ್ದ ಹಾಗೆ ಹೇಳು	**idda hâge hêḷu**
Tell the exact truth	which was like tell
ಇದ್ದದ್ದಿರಲಿ	**iddad'**[2] **irali**
Let it be as it is	that which was let it be
ಇಲ್ಲಿರ ಬಾರದು	**ill' ira bâradu**[3]
You (*a. p.*) must not remain here	here to be it will not come

13. ಇರು iru (*continued*).

Negative Mood (present and future, sometimes past).

Verbal participle, **irade, illade,** not being
Relative participle, **irada, illada,** (that) which is not, (they) who are not
Verbal Noun, **iradu, illaddu,** the not being, that which is not

Singular:		*Plural:*	
ire(nu), *or* **illa,**	I am not	**ir-evu,** *or* **illa,**	we are not
ir-e, *or* **illa,**	thou art not	**ir-ari,** *or* **illa,**	you are not
ir-a(nu), *or* **illa,**	he is not	**ir-aru,** *or* **illa,**	they (*m. & f.*) are not
ir-aḷu, *or* **illa,**	she is not	**ir-avu,** *or* **illa,**	they (*n.*) are not
ir-adu, *or* **illa,**	it is not		

Remarks:—1. The root *il*, of which the above forms illa, illade, and illada are made, is an old form of *ir* (*iru*); but in the Negative Mood the forms derived from *il* are more in use than those derived from *iru*.

2. In forming the Negative Mood, the terminations *e* (*nu*), *e*, *a* (*nu*), *a* (*ḷu*), etc. are joined to the crude form, omitting the final *u* in the case of verbs

---

1 *Idd'illa—iddu+illa*, see Remark 3 to the Negative Mood No. 13.

2 Past Verbal noun of *iru*; as to its meaning see *bandaddu* p. 12, No. 2.

3 *Bâradu* is 3rd person, neuter, singular of the negative mood of *baru*, see No. 13.

ending in *u*, and inserting the consonant *y* in the case of verbs ending in *e*, *i*, *â*, *ô*, *û*; as, hôgu; Negative Mood, hôge or hôgenu; âgu, âge, or âgenu; kare, kareyenu; bari, bariyenu. The Negative Mood of baru and taru is b'ârenu, târenu.

3. The Negative Mood is colloquially not much used now, excepting the participle and the verbal noun; in its stead the following compound forms are common—

a) for the present tense, the present verbal noun with illa; as, nânu hôguvadilla; see note 4, p. 13;

b) for the past tense the infinitive ending in *lu* with *illa*, for the perfect tense the past verbal participle with *illa*; as, nânu band'illa, nânu baralilla, see note 2, p. 14;

c) for the future tense, the infinitive ending in *likke* with *illa;* as, nânu baralikkilla, etc., or else, the same as for the present tense.

ನನಗೆ ಕೆಲಸಿಲ್ಲ (ಕೆಲಸವಿಲ್ಲ)	**nanage kelas' illa (kelasa-v-illa)**[1]
I have no work	to me work is not (work is not)
ಯಾರು ಬಂದರು? ಯಾರೂ ಇಲ್ಲ	**yâru bandaru? yâr'û illa**
Who is come? No one	who came? who even not
ಏನಿಲ್ಲ, ಏನೂ ಇಲ್ಲ	**yên' illa, yên'û illa**
Nothing, nothing at all	what is not, what even is not
ನೀವುಣ್ಣುವದಿಲ್ಲ	**nîv' uṇṇuvad' illa**
You don't eat	you the eating is not
ಆಕೆ ಉಂಡಿಲ್ಲ (ಉಣ್ಣಲಿಲ್ಲ *C.*)	**âke uṇḍ' illa (uṇṇal' illa *C.*)**
She has not dined	she h. eaten is not (to eat is not)
ಆಕೆ ಉಣ್ಣಲಿಕ್ಕಿಲ್ಲ	**âke uṇṇalikk' illa**
She will (probably) not eat	she to eat is not
ಇಲ್ಲದ ಮಾತಾಡ ಬೇಡ	**illada mât' âḍa bêḍa**
Don't tell lies; ...stories	which is not word to play is not wanted
ಇನ್ನೂ ಬಂದಿಲ್ಲ (ಬರಲಿಲ್ಲ *C.*)	**inn'û band' illa (baral'illa *C.*)**
He (*a.p.*) is not yet come	yet even h. come is not (to come is not)
ನನಗೆ ಅನ್ನವಿಲ್ಲ, ನೀರಿಲ್ಲ, ಏನೂ ಇಲ್ಲ	**nanage annavilla[2], nîr'illa, yên'û illa**
I have neither rice, nor water, nor anything; I have nothing to eat	to me rice is not, water is not, what even is not
ಇಲ್ಲವೇ ಇಲ್ಲ, ಇಲ್ಲೇ ಇಲ್ಲ	**illa-v-ê illa, ill'ê illa**
Not at all	not (*emph.*) not, not (*emph.*)

---

[1] See note 2, p. 20.

[2] People of lower ranks use the word *kûlu*= cooked rice, food, instead of *anna*.

14. ಅಲ್ಲ **alla** = it is not so, it is not fit, not (*G. es ist nicht so, es ist unpassend, nicht*).

This defective verb is derived from the old root *al*, to be fit or proper, of which only the following four forms of the Negative Mood are still in common use—

Present tense,	**alla,**	I am not fit, thou art not fit; or it is not I, thou, he, etc. (used in all numbers and persons)
Verbal participle,	**allade,**	not being fit, being unfit, being not so, besides
Relative,	**allada,**	who or which is unfit, . . . is not so
Verbal noun,	**alladdu,**	that which is unfit, . . . improper

---

ಅದಲ್ಲ, ಇದು	**ad' alla, idu**
Not that, but this	that not this
ಇದು ನನ್ನದಲ್ಲ	**idu nannad'[1] alla**
This is not mine	this mine is not
ಇದು ಒಳ್ಳೇದಲ್ಲ	**idu wol̤l̤êd'[1] alla**
This is not good; this is not a [good one	this good one is not
ಇದು ಚಲೋ ಮನೆಯಲ್ಲ	**idu čalô mane-y-alla**
This is not a nice house	this nice house not
ನೀವು ಒಳ್ಳೆಯವರಲ್ಲ	**nîvu wol̤l̤e-y-avar' alla**
You are not good	you good ones not
ಅವ(ನು) ಬಂದನಲ್ಲಾ? (ಅಲ್ಲವೋ? *C.*)	**ava(nu) bandan' allâ[2]? (alla-v-ô[3]? *C.*)**
He has come, has he not?	he came not? (not?)
ಇದು ಅಲ್ಲದ ಕೆಲಸ	**idu allada kelasa**
This is an improper thing	this improper business
ಅಲ್ಲವೋ? *C.* ಹೌದಲ್ಲೋ? *S.*	**alla-v-ô[3]? haud' allô?**
Is it not? is it not so?	not? yes not?
ಇದಲ್ಲದೆ, ಅದಲ್ಲದೆ	**id' allade, ad' allade**
Besides this, ... that	this not being so, that not being so
ಇವನನ್ನಲ್ಲ, ಅವನನ್ನು ಕರೆ	**ivanann' alla, avanannu kare**
Call that man (boy), not this	this man not, that man call

---

[1] See Remark 2, No. 6. In Mysore and S. Kanara *wol̤l̤e*=good, is used for things as well as persons, in the S. Maharatta districts *wol̤l̤e* is only used for moral goodness, *čalô* for nice, fine, good, when used of things.

[2] The lengthened sound â at the end of *allâ*, gives to this word the force of a query: "is it not so?"

[3] *Allavô*, is *alla* with the interrogative particle *ô*, and the consonant *v* inserted for euphony's sake.

15. ಬೇಕು bêku=it is wanted, must, should, ought (*French, il faut*).

Remarks:—1. Bêku, originally bêḍkum, is probably derived from the root bêḍu, to ask, beg, desire and is an Old Kanarese form ending in *kum* or *ku*, which was formerly used for the 3rd person of both numbers, in all three genders and tenses. The meaning would appear originally to have been, he, she or it asks, requests, desires; bêḍa (see No. 16) seems to be a form of the Negative Mood of the same root.

2. Bêku, when combined with âgu forms a verb which may be conjugated like âgu; as, bêkâguttade, it is wanted, required.

ನನಗೆ ನೀರು ಬೇಕು	**nanage nîru bêku**
I want some water	to me water is wanted
ಬೇಕಾದರೆ ಕೊಡುತ್ತೇನೆ	**bêk' âdare[1] koḍuttêne**
If you wish, I shall give you some	it is wanted if become I give
ಇನ್ನೂ ಬೇಕು	**inn'û bêku**
I want some more	still even (it) is wanted
ಯಾವಾಗ ಬರ ಬೇಕು?	**yâvâga bara bêku?**
When am I (*a. p.*) to come?	when to come is wanted
ಮೂರು ಘಂಟೆಗೆ ಬರ ಬೇಕು	**mûru ghaṇṭege bara bêku**
Come at three o'clock; let him (*a. p.*) come, *etc.*	three to bell to come is wanted
ಬರಲಿಕ್ಕೇ ಬೇಕಾಗುವದಿಲ್ಲ	**baralikkê bêkâguvad' illa**
You (*a. p.*) need not come; it is not necessary to come	to come (*emph.*) is wanted not
ಅನ್ನ ಬೇಕೇನು? *S.* (.. ಬೇಕೋ? *C.*)	**anna bêk' ênu?** *S.* (...**bêkô?** *C.*)
Do you want some rice?	rice is wanted what? (... is wanted?)
ಬೇಕಾಗಿಲ್ಲ	**bêkâg' illa**
I don't want any	h. been wanted it is not
ಬೇಕಾದದ್ದೆಲ್ಲಾ ತಾ	**bêkâdd'[2] ellâ tâ**
Bring everything necessary	that which is wanted all bring
ಬೇಕಾದಷ್ಟದೆ *S.*, ಬೇಕಾದಷ್ಟುಂಟು *C.*	[*C.* **bêkâd'ashṭ'ade** *S.*, **bêkâd'ashṭuṇṭu**
There is as much as is wanted; 2. there is plenty	that is wanted, so much is

---

[1] The conditional particle *re*=if, is affixed to the relative p. p. in the interlineary translation, its equivalent *if* will always be placed before the p. p.

[2] *Bêk'âdaddu;* for this form *âdaddu* of the past verbal noun the abbreviated form *âddu* is much used, especially in compounds.

16. ಬೇಡ bêḍa (often pronounced byâḍa) = it is not wanted (*French, il ne faut pas*). [bêḍa

ಇದು ನನಗೆ ಬೇಡ, ಅವನು ನನಗೆ ಬೇಡ	**idu nanage bêḍa, avanu nanage**
I don't want this, ... him	this to me is not wanted, he to me is not wanted
ಏನೂ ಬೇಡ	**yên'û bêḍa**
I don't want anything	what even is not wanted
ಅವರು ಬೇಡಂದರೆ ನನಗೆ ಕೊಡು	**avaru bêḍ' andare nanage koḍu**
If they don't want it, give it to me	they it is not wanted if said to me give
ಬೇಡಾದರೆ ಏನು ಮಾಡಲಿ?	**bêḍ' âdare yênu mâḍali?**
If you (he, *etc.*) don't want it, I can't help it	not wanted if become what let me (*a.p.*) do
ನೀ ಬರ ಬೇಡ, ಅವನು ಬರಲಿ	**nî bara bêḍa, avanu barali**
You need not come, let him come	thou to come is not wanted, let him come
ಈಗ ಮಲಗಿಕೊಳ್ಳಬೇಡ	**îga malagikoḷḷa[1] bêḍa**
Don't go to bed yet	now to lie down is not wanted
ದೂರ ಹೋಗ ಬೇಡಿರಿ	**dûra hôga bêḍiri** (*pl.*)
Don't go far	far to go is not wanted
ಇವರು ನಿಮಗೇನಾಗಬೇಕು?	**ivaru nimag'ên' âga bêku?**
How are you related to them (.. him)?	these to you what to become is wanted
ಏನೂ ಆಗ ಬಾರದು	**yên'û âga bâradu[2]**
We are not related	what even to become it will not come
ಅವರು ನಮ್ಮ ಮಕ್ಕಳು	**avaru namma makkaḷu[3]**
They are our children	they our children

17. ಕೊಳ್ಳು koḷḷu = to take, to buy (*G. sich aneignen*).

Past verbal participle,	**koṇḍu**
,, *relative* ,,	**koṇḍa**
Past tense 3rd pers. neut. singular,	**koṇḍitu**

Remarks:—1. The different forms of this verb are frequently added to the past verbal participle of other verbs, to signify that an action is performed for the bene-

---

[1] About the use of this verb see No. 17.

[2] See note 3, p. 25.

[3] Plural of *magu*, see No. 65.

fit or to the damage of the agent himself. Reflexive verbs are generally translated with compounds of this verb, and its meaning is therefore often expressed in English by adding the word *himself* or *herself* as an object. But frequently the shade of meaning is so slight that it cannot be translated in English.

2. In the composition of the past verbal participle (p. v. p.) with koḷḷu or its different forms, the last syllable of the p. v. p. is often dropped; as, karedu or karadu (p. v. p. of kare=to call)+koḷḷu, becomes karakoḷḷu, tegadu or tegedu (p. v. p. of tegi)+koḷḷu becomes tekkoḷḷu or takkoḷḷu.

ಒಂದು ಕುದುರೆ ಕೊಳ್ಳ ಬೇಕು, ಕೊಳ್ಳಲಿಕ್ಕೆ ಬೇಕು	**wondu kudure koḷḷa bêku, koḷḷalikke bêku**
I (*a. p.*) must buy a horse	one horse to buy is wanted
ಎಲ್ಲಿ ಕೊಂಡಿರಿ?	**yelli koṇḍiri?**
Where did you buy it?	where you took
ಮಲಗಿಕೊಂಡಿರುತ್ತಾರೆ	**malagi koṇḍ' iruttâre**
They are in bed, they are asleep	h. lain down h. taken they are
ಬರ(ದು)ಕೊಳ್ಳುತ್ತಾನೆ	**bara(du)[1] koḷḷuttâne**
He is writing; he will write it	h. written he takes
ಅವರನ್ನು ಕರಕೊಂಡು ಬಾ	**avarannu kara' koṇḍu bâ**
Call them (him) here	them h. called h. taken come
ಅವರಿಗೆ ಹೇಳಿಕೊಳ್ಳ ಬೇಕು	**avarige[2] hêḷi koḷḷa bêku**
You should speak to him (confess to him, entreat him)	to them h. told to take is wanted
ತೆಗೆದುಕೋ, ತಕ್ಕೋ	**tegedukô, takkô**
Take it (for yourself)	h. taken, take
ಎಲ್ಲಿಟ್ಟುಕೊಂಡಳು?	**yell' iṭṭu[3] koṇḍaḷu?**
Where did she keep it?	where h. put she took
ಒಂದು ಕತ್ತಿ ಮಾಡಿಕೊಂಡ	**wondu katti mâḍi koṇḍa**
He made himself a knife (sword)	one knife h. made he took
ಇಲ್ಲ, ಮಾಡಿಸಿಕೊಂಡ	**illa, mâḍisi[4] koṇḍa**
No, he got it made	not, h. caused to make he took

---

1 *Baradu* p. v. p. of *bari*=to write.

2 The use of the plural for the singular in an honorary way is very common in Kanarese, not only in the 2nd person but also in the 1st and 3rd persons.

3 *Iṭṭu* p. v. p. of *iḍu*.

4 The termination *isu* or *su* added to the crude form of a verb, gives it a causative meaning; the last letter of the verb is, as usually before a vowel, dropped.

18. ತೆಗಿ tegi or ತೆಗೆ tege = to take, to remove (*G. nehmen, wegnehmen*).

Conjugation of verbs ending in *e* or *i*.

Present verbal participle,	**tegi-y-utta** or **tege-y-utta,** taking
Present (& future) relat. part.,	**tegi-y-uva,** „ **tege-y-uva** (he) who takes (that) which „
Infinitive,	**tegi-y-a, tegi-y-alu, tegi-y-a-likke,** or **tege-y-a, tege-y-alu, tege-y-a-likke,** } to take
Verbal noun,	**tegi-y-uvadu,** or **tege-y-uvadu,** the taking
Present tense,	**tegi-y-uttêne,** or **tege-y-uttêne,** I take etc. etc. etc. *as in* **baru**
Imperative singular,	**tegi** or **tege,** take **tegi-y-ali,** or **tege-y-ali,** let me (him, her, it, them) take
„ *plural,*	**tegi-y-iri, tege-y-iri,** take
Past verbal participle,	**tege-du, tega-du,** having taken
„ *relative* „	**tege-da, tega-da,** (he) who took, (that) which took
„ *verbal noun,*	**tege-ddu,** or **tega-da-ddu,** the h. taken, that which has been taken
Past tense,	**tege-de (nu),** I took etc.
3rd person neuter,	**tege-y-itu**
1st Future tense,	**teged-ênu, teged-î, teged-ânu,** etc.

Negative Mood.

Verbal participle,	**tegi-y-ade, tege-y-ade,** not taking
Relative participle,	**tegi-y-ada, tege-y-ada,** (he) who *or* (that) which does not take, *or* has not taken
Verbal noun,	**tegi-y-addu, tege-y-addu,** the not having taken, that which is not taken

tegi-y-e(nu), or **tege-y-e(nu),** I do not take, shall not take
tegi-y-e or **tege-y-e,** thou dost not take
etc. etc. *as in No. 3.*

Remark:—The terminal letter *i* frequently interchanges with *e*, or (in the past participle and past tense) with *a*. Some roots however retain the *i*.

ಅದನ್ನು ತೆಗಿ	**adannu tegi**
Take that away	that take
ಇದನ್ನು ತೆಗಿಯ ಬೇಡ	**idannu tegiya bêḍa**
Don't take this away [ಹೋಗು	this to take is not wanted [**hôgu**[1]
ಕೊಡೆ ತೆಗೆದುಕೊಂಡು (ತಕ್ಕೊಂಡು)	**koḍe tegedukoṇḍu (takkoṇḍu)**
Take an umbrella	umbrella h. taken go
ಅಕ್ಕಿ ತೆಗೆದುಕೊಂಡು (ತಕ್ಕೊಂಡು) ಬಾ	**akki tegedukoṇḍu (takkoṇḍu) bâ**
Bring some rice	rice having taken come
ಆ ಕತ್ತಿ ಯಾಕೆ ತಕ್ಕೊಂಡಿ?	**â katti yâke takkoṇḍi?**
Why did you take that knife?	that knife why thou tookst
ನಾ ತಕ್ಕೊಳ್ಳಲಿಲ್ಲ, ಅವನು ತಕ್ಕೊಂಡ	**nâ takkoḷḷal'illa, avanu takkoṇḍa**
I did not take it, he took it	I to take is not, he took
ನಾ ಯಾಕೆ ತಕ್ಕೊಳ್ಳಲಿ?	**nâ yâke takkoḷḷali?**
Why should I take it?	I why let (*a.p.*) take
ಇದಕ್ಕೇನು ತಕ್ಕೊಳ್ಳುತ್ತೀರಿ?	**idakk' ênu takkoḷḷuttîri?**
What will you take for this? what is the price of this?	to this what you take
ನೀವು ಕೊಟ್ಟಷ್ಟು ತಕ್ಕೊಳ್ಳುತ್ತೇನೆ [me	**nîvu koṭṭ'**[2] **ashṭu takkoḷḷuttêne**
I shall take as much as you give	you which gave so much I take
ಬಾಗಲು ತೆಗೆದರಂತೆ	**bâgalu tegedar' ante**
The door has been opened, I hear	door they took away it says

19. ಕೈ kei = hand (*G. Hand*).

Declension of Nouns ending in *i* or *e*.

	Singular:	*Plural:*
1. Nom.	**kei-y-u**, the hand	**kei-gaḷu**, the hands
2. Acc.	**kei-y-annu**, the hand	**kei-gaḷ-annu**, the hands
3. Instr.	**kei-y-inda**, by, from, or with the h.	**kei-gaḷ-inda**, by, from, with the hands
4. Dat.	**kei-ge**, to the hand	**kei-gaḷ-ige**, to the hands
6. Gen.	**kei-y-a**, of ,, ,,	**kei-gaḷ-a**, of ,, ,,
7. Loc.	**kei-y-alli**, in the hand	**kei-gaḷ-alli**, in ,, ,,

1 *Tegedukoṇḍu hôgu* or *takkoṇḍu hôgu*, literally, having taken to go, signifies to take away; *tegedukoṇḍu* (or *takkoṇḍu*) *baru*, to bring.

2 For *koṭṭa*, rel. past participle of *koḍu*.

Remarks:—1. In the same way all neuter nouns, and the singular of all masculine and feminine ending in *e* or *i* are declined; as, m a n e - y - u, m a n e - y - a n n u, m a n e - y - i n d a, m a n e - g e, e t c.

2. As to the plural of masculine and feminine nouns ending in *e* or *i* see No. 64.

ನಿನಗೆಷ್ಟು ಕೈ?	**ninag' eshṭu kei?**
How many hands have you?	to thee how many hand?
ನನಗೆರಡು ಕೈ	**nanag' eraḍu kei**
I have two hands	to me two hand
ನಿನ್ನ ಕೈ ತೋರಿಸು	**ninna kei[1] tôrisu**
Show me your hand (hands)	thy hand make appear
ನನ್ನ ಕೈಯಿಂದಾಗುವದಿಲ್ಲ	**nanna keiyind' âguvad' illa**
I cannot do it	my by hand the being done is not
ನಿಮ್ಮ ಕೈಕೆಳಗಿರುತ್ತಾನೆ	**nimma kei[2] keḷag' iruttâne**
He is under your authority	your hand under he is
ಈ ಮಾತು ನಿಮ್ಮ ಕೈಯಲ್ಲಿ ಅದೆ	**î mâtu nimma keiyalli ade**
This matter is in your hands	this word your in hand is
ಅವನ ಕೈಯಲ್ಲಿ ಆಗದು (...ಕೈಲಾಗದು)	**avana keiyalli âgadu[3] (keil' âgadu)**
He cannot do it	his in hand it will not become
ಅವನು ಕೈಲಾಗದವ	**avanu keil' âgad'[4] ava**
He is a good-for-nothing fellow	he in hand which is not done he
ಇದರಲ್ಲಿ ಕೈಹಾಕ ಬೇಡ	**idaralli kei hâka bêḍa**
Don't interfere in it	in this hand to throw is not wanted
ಯಾಕದರಲ್ಲಿ ಕೈ ಹಾಕಿದಿ?	**yâk' adaralli kei hâkidi?**
Why did you thrust your hand into it? Why did you interfere?	why in that hand threwest?

---

[1] The crude form for the accusative case. In colloquial language the accusative case is seldom used except to avoid ambiguity.

[2] The crude form instead of the genitive case *keiya*.

[3] *Keiyalli*, in old Kanarese *keyîli*, colloquially abbreviated into *keili*. *Âgadu* is 3rd pers. neut. sing. of the negative mood of *âgu;* See No. 13.

[4] *keil'âgad'ava=keyîli-âgad-ava;* the nominative "anything" to the verb *âgada* is understood. The meaning is therefore "he or one by whose hands nothing is done, a good-for-nothing fellow". *Âgada* is the negative relative participle.

20. ನಾವು nâvu[1]=we (*G. wir*). See No. 7.

ನಾವಿಲ್ಲದೆ ಏನು ಮಾಡುವಿರಿ?	nâv'illade yênu mâḍuviri?
What will you do without us (me)?	we not being what you will do?
ನಮ್ಮ ಮನೆಗೆ ಬರ್ರಿ *S.* (ಬನ್ನಿ *C.*)	namma manege barri *S.* (banni *C.*)
Come to my house	our to house come
ಈ ಮನೆ ನಮ್ಮದು	î mane nammadu
This is my house	this house ours [(band'illa)
ನಮ್ಮವರು ಇನ್ನೂ ಬರಲಿಲ್ಲ (ಬಂದಿಲ್ಲ *S.*)	namm'avaru inn'û baral'illa
Our people are not yet come	our they yet even to come is not
My husband[2] is not yet come	(h. come is not)
ನಮ್ಮನ್ನು ಯಾಕೆ ಕರೆಯಲಿಲ್ಲ?	nammannu yâke kareyal'illa?
Why did you not call us (me)?	us why to call is not?
ನಮಗೆ ಕೇಳ ಬೇಡ	namage kêḷa bêḍa
Do not ask it of us (me)	to us to ask is not wanted
ನಮಗೆ ಕೇಳಿಸುವದಿಲ್ಲ	namage kêḷisuvad'[3] illa
We (I) cannot hear it	to us the causing to hear is not
ನಮಗೆ ಸಾಕಾಯಿತು	namage sâk' âyitu[4]
I have enough (of it)	to us enough it became
ನಮ್ಮಲ್ಲಿ ಕೆಲಸಿಲ್ಲ (ಕೆಲಸವಿಲ್ಲ)	nammalli kelas'illa (kelasa-v-illa)
We (I) have no work for you	in us work is not (work is not)
ನಮ್ಮಲ್ಲಿರ ಬಹುದು	nammall'ira bahudu[5]
You (*a. p.*) may stay with us	in us to be it will come

---

1 *Nâvu* is very frequently used for the 1st person singular in an honorary way; people of some standing generally speak of themselves in the plural.

2 *Nammavaru* is often used by native women when speaking of their husbands, while the husband, when speaking of his wife, says "*nammâke*".

3 About the termination *isu* see Note 4, p. 30. The nominative is understood; it may be supposed to be "some sound", and the literal meaning is, "(that sound) does not cause my ear to hear it".

4 *Sâku* (instead of *sâlku*) is an old form of the verb *sâlu*, signifying, "it is (there is) enough". Compare Rem. 1 to No. 15.

5 *Bahudu* (it will come) is an old form of the 3rd pers. neut. singular of the second future tense (see No. 38) of *baru*, now only used after the infinitive mood of another verb in the sense of "it is possible". It may generally be rendered by the auxiliary *can* or *may*, but it is used with all persons, genders and numbers; as, *nân'ira bahudu*= I can stay, *âke ira bahudu*=She may stay, *avaru ira bahudu*=they may stay.

The corresponding negative form *bâradu* (it will not come) is used in the same way to express prohibition; as, *nîvu bara bâradu*=you may not come, you are not permitted to come.

21. ನೀವು **nîvu**=you (*G. ihr*). See. No. 7, Rem. 1.

ನೀವು ಯಾರು?	**nîvu yâru?**
Who are you?	you who?
ನಿಮ್ಮನ್ನು ಎಂದೂ ನೋಡಲಿಲ್ಲ (ನೋಡಿದ್ದಿಲ್ಲ *S.*)	**nimmannu yendû nôḍal'illa (nôḍidd'illa** *S.*) [h. seen is not)
I have never seen you before	you (*acc.*) when even to see is not (the
ನಿಮ್ಮಿಂದ ಕುದುರೆ ಕೊಂಡುಕೊಂಡೆವಲ್ಲಾ?	**nimminda kudure koṇḍukoṇḍev' alla?**
Did we (I) not buy a horse of you?	from you horse h. taken we took not?
ನಿಮಗೆ ಮನೆ ಇಲ್ಲೇನು? (ಇಲ್ಲವೋ?)	**nimage mane ill'ênu?** *S.* **(illa-v-ô?** *C.*)
Have you got no house?	to you house is not what? (is not?)
ನಿಮಗೆಷ್ಟು ಮಂದಿ ಮಕ್ಕಳು?	**nimag' eshṭu mandi makkaḷu?**
How many children have you?	to you how many children?
ನಿಮಗೆ ಗೊತ್ತಿಲ್ಲ	**nimage gott' illa**
You do not know	to you certainly is not
ನಿಮ್ಮ ಮುಂದೆ ಏನು ಹೇಳಲಿ?	**nimma muṇde yênu hêḷali?**
What shall (can) I say to you?	your before what let me say?
ನಿಮ್ಮದು ನಮಗೆ ಬೇಡ	**nimmadu namage bêḍa**
We (I) don't want your things	yours to us is not wanted
ನಿಮ್ಮಲ್ಲಿ ಯಾರಾದರೂ ಹೋಗಲಿ	**nimmalli yâr'âdar'û**[1] **hôgali**
Let some one of you go	in you any one let go
ನಿಮ್ಮಂಥವರಿಗೆ ಯಾರು ರೂಪಾಯಿ ಕೊಟ್ಟಾರು?	**nimm'anth'avarige yâru rûpâyi koṭṭâru?**
Who will give money to such as you?	your such to them who rupee they will give

22. ಕೆಲಸ **kelasa**=work, business (*G. Geschäft, Arbeit*).

Declensions of Neuter Nouns ending in a.

	Singular:	*Plural:*
1. Nom.	**kelasa-vu**, the work	**kelasa-gaḷ-u**, the works
2. Acc.	**kelasa-v-annu**, the work	**kelasa-gaḷ-annu**, the works
3. Inst.	**kelasa-d-inda**, by, from, or with the work	**kelasa-gaḷ-inda**, by, from, or with work
4. Dat.	**kelasa-kke**, to the work	**kelasa-gaḷ-ige**, to the works
6. Gen.	**kelasa-d-a**, of the work	**kelasa-gaḷ-a**, of „ „
7. Loc.	**kelasa-d-alli**, in the work	**kelasa-gaḷ-alli**, in „ „

[1] *Yâru*+*âda*+*re*+*û*=whosoever it be, any one; see No. 51.

ನನಗೆ ಬಹಳ ಕೆಲಸ; ನನ್ನ ಕೆಲಸ ಬಹಳ	**nanage bahaḷa kelasa; nanna kelasa bahaḷa**
I have much work; I have a great deal to do	to me much work; my work much
ಇದು ಯಾತರ ಕೆಲಸ?	**idu yâtara[1] kelasa?**
What kind of work is this?	this of which the work?
ಇಂಥಾ ಕೆಲಸ ಮಾಡ ಬೇಡ	**inthâ kelasa mâḍa bêḍa**
Don't do such a thing as this	such work to do is not wanted
ಹೇಳಿದ ಕೆಲಸ ಮಾಡು	**hêḷida kelasa[2] mâḍu**
Do what you have been told to do	which told work do
ಈ ಕೆಲಸದಿಂದ ಏನಾಗುತ್ತದೆ? [matter?	**î kelasadinda yên' âguttade?**
What will be the result (use) of this	this from work what it becomes?
ನಿನ್ನ ಕೆಲಸ ಯಾಕೆ ಬಿಟ್ಟುಬಂದಿ?	**ninna kelasa yâke biṭṭu[3] bandi?**
Why have you left your work?	thy work why h. left camest?
ನಿನ್ನ ಕೆಲಸಕ್ಕೆ ಹೋಗು (ಕೆಲಸಕ್ಹೋಗು)	**ninna kelaskke hôgu (kelasak' hôgu[4])**
Go to your work	thy to work go
ಇದು ಕೆಲಸಕ್ಕೆ ಬರುವದಿಲ್ಲ	**idu kelasakke baruvad' illa**
It is of no use	this to work the coming is not
ಹಗಲೆಲ್ಲಾ ಕೆಲಸದಲ್ಲಿರಬೇಕು [all day	**hagal'ellâ kelasadall'ira bêku**
I (*a. p.*) am obliged to be at work	day all in work to be is wanted
ಕೆಲಸಾದ ಮೇಲೆ ಬಾ	**kelas'âda mêle bâ**
Come when your work is over	work after being done come

23. ಊರು **ûru** = town, village (*G. Stadt, Dorf*).

Conjugated like **mâtu** (No. 5), but instead of **ûrininda, ûrina, ûrinalli,** the forms **ûrinda, ûra, ûralli** are used optionally.

ಇದು ಯಾವ ಊರು? ಯಾವ ಊರಿದು?	**idu yâva ûru? yâva ûr' idu?**
What town is this?	this what town? what town this?
ಇದು ಮಂಗಳೂರು	**idu Maṅgaḷûru**
This is Mangalore	this Mangalore

---

1 *Yâtara* instead of *yâvadara*, genitive case of *yâvadu* = *yâva* + *du*, signifying, "of what kind"; *yâtara kelasa* = "what kind of work".

2 *Hêḷida kelasa* properly means, the work which told; but the nominative I (or some one else) being understood, it signifies "the work which I (or some one else) told you".

3 *Biṭṭu* is verbal participle of *biḍu*; see No. 45.

4 The form within the brackets is the only one used colloquially.

ಇದು ದೊಡ್ಡ ಊರು	**idu doḍḍa ûru**
It is a big place (town, village)	this great town
ಈ ಊರು ದೊಡ್ಡದು	**î ûru doḍḍadu**
This town is large	this town large one
ನೀವು ಯಾವ ಊರಿನವರು? (ಊರವರು?)	**nîvu yâva ûrin'avaru? (ûr'avaru?)**
What is your native place?	you what of town they (of town they)?
ನಮ್ಮೂರು ಧಾರವಾಡ	**namm'ûru dhâravâḍa**
We are of Dharwar	our town Dharwar
ಊರಿಗೆ ಹೋದನು	**ûrige hôdanu**
He went abroad	to town he went
ಯಾವ ಊರಿನಿಂದ (ಊರಿಂದ) ಬಂದಿರಿ?	**yâva ûrininda (ûrinda) bandiri?**
From what place have you come?	what from town you came?
ಊರಲ್ಲಿರುತ್ತಾರೆ	**ûrall' iruttâre**
They are (live) in the town (he is..)	in town they are
ಅವರು ಊರಲ್ಲಿಲ್ಲ	**avaru ûrall' illa**
They are not in town (he is..)	they in town not

24. ಮನೆ **mane** = house, family, room, partition (of a box, *etc.*)
(*G. Hause, Familie, Zimmer, Fach.*)

ಇದು ಯಾರ ಮನೆ? ಈ ಮನೆ ಯಾರದು?	**idu yâra mane? î mane yâradu[1]?**
Whose house is this?	this whose house? this house whose?
ಇದು ನಮ್ಮ ಮನೆ	**idu namma mane**
This is my house	this our house
ಮನೆಯಿಂದ ಬಂದ	**maneyinda banda**
He has come from home	from the house he came
ಮನೆಗೆ ಹೋಗು	**manege hôgu**
Go home	to the house go
ನಿಮ್ಮ ಮನೆಯವರೆಲ್ಲರೂ ಬರಲಿ	**nimma maney'avar'ellar'û barali**
Let all the members of your family [come	your house's they all even let come
ನಿಮ್ಮ ಮನೆಯವರು ಹ್ಯಾಗಿರುತ್ತಾರೆ?	**nimma maney'avaru hyâg'-iruttâre?**
How are your family?	your house's they how they are?
ಮನೆಯಲ್ಲಿರುತ್ತಾರೆ	**maneyall' iruttâre**
They are at home (he is...)	in the house they are

[1] See p. 18, Remark 2.

ಅವನು ಮನೆಯಲ್ಲಿಲ್ಲ	avanu maneyall' illa
He is not at home	he in the house is not
ಮನೆಯೊಳಗೆ ಕೊಡು	maneyoḷage[1] koḍu
Give it to my wife (to your mother)	in the house give
ಕುದುರೇ ಮನೆ, ಎತ್ತಿನ ಮನೆ	kudurê[2] mane, yettina mane
A stable, an ox stall	horse's house, ox's house

25. ಬಾಗಲ, ಬಾಗಲು **bâgala, bâgalu**[3]=door (*G. Tur*).

ಈ ಮನೆಗೆ ಒಂದೇ ಬಾಗಲು (-ಲ)	**î manege *w*ondê bâgalu (-la)**
This house has only one door	this to house *one* door [(-gaḷu)
ನಮ್ಮ ಮನೆಗೆ ಮೂರು ಬಾಗಲು (-ಗಳು)	**namma manege mûru bâgalu**
My house has three doors	our to house three door (-s)
ಬಾಗಲಿನ (ಬಾಗಲ) ಮುಂದೆ ಮಲಗುತ್ತಾನೆ	**bâgalina (bagala) munde malaguttâne**
He sleeps before the door	of the door before he lies
ಬಾಗಲು (ಬಾಗಲ) ಹಾಕಿದ ಮೇಲೆ ಬಂದ	**bâgalu (bâgala) hâkida mêle banda**
He came after the door had been shut	door which is put after he came
ಬಾಗಲು ತೆಗಿ (ಬಾಗಲ...)	**bâgalu tegi (bâgala...)**
Open the door [ಮುಚ್ಚು	door take [**mučču**
ಬಾಗಲು ಹಾಕು (ಬಾಗಲ...); ಬಾಗಲು	**bâgalu hâku (bâgala...); bâgalu-**
Shut the door	door throw; door shut
ನಮ್ಮ ಬಾಗಲಿಗೆ ಬರ ಬೇಡ	**namma bâgalige bara bêda**
Don't come to my door	our to door to come is not wanted
ಈ ಬಾಗಲಿನಿಂದ (ಬಾಗಲದಿಂದ) ಹೋಗು	**î bâgalininda (bâgaladinda) hôgu**
Go away from this door	this from door go
ಬಾಗಲಿನ (ಬಾಗಲದ) ಮೇಲೆ ಬರೆಯ ಬೇಡ	**bâgalina(bâgalada)mêle bareya bêḍa**
Don't write on the door	of the door on to write is not wanted
ಬಾಗಲುಗಳೆಲ್ಲಾ ಹಾಕಿವೆ;... ಮುಚ್ಚಿವೆ	**bâgalugaḷ' ellâ hâk'ive[4],..mučč'ive**
All the doors are shut	doors all h. put they are; shut they are

[1] The reluctance of Hindus to name their wives is well known; they prefer using some other term; a father when speaking to his child of its mother will generally use the expression above mentioned.

[2] The genitive case of nouns ending in *e* or *i* which ends in *eya, iya* is often formed only by lengthening the last letter, as *ê* or *î*.

[3] The form of *bâgala*, genitive *bâgalada* or only *bâgala* is more common in Southern Mahratta; *bagalu*, genitive *bâgalina* on the coast.

[4] *Hâki*, verbal participle; *ive* = *ave*, 3rd person, neuter gender, plural of *iru*; see No. 11, Rem.

26. ಘಂಟೆ Ghaṇṭe=bell, hour (*G. Clocke*).

ಘಂಟೆ ಬಾರಿಸು	**ghaṇṭe bârisu**
Ring the bell	bell ring
ಎಷ್ಟು ಘಂಟೆ (ಆಯಿತು)?	***y*eshṭu ghaṇṭe (âyitu?)**
What o'clock is it?	how many bell (it became)?
ಮೂರು ಘಂಟೆ ಆಗಿ ಹೋಯಿತು	**mûru ghaṇṭe âgi hôyitu**
It is past three o'clock	three bell h. become it went
ಎಷ್ಟು ಘಂಟೆಗೆ ಬರಲಿ?	***y*eshṭu ghaṇṭege barali?**
At what o'clock am I to come (is he, are we, are they to come)?	how many to bell let (*a.p.*) come?
ನಾಲ್ಕು ಘಂಟೆಯ ಮೇಲೆ	**nâlku ghaṇṭeya mêle**
After four o'clock	four of the bell after
ಇನ್ನೂ ಒಂದು ಘಂಟೆಯಾಗಿಲ್ಲ *S.*, ಆಗಲಿಲ್ಲ *C.*	**innû *w*ondu ghaṇṭe-y-âg'illa *S.*, âgal'illa *C.***
It is not yet one o'clock	yet even one bell h. become is not, ...to become is not
ಐದು ಘಂಟೆಯಾದಾಗ ಹೇಳು	**eidu ghaṇṭe-y-âd' âga hêḷu**
When it is five o'clock let me know	five bell which became then tell
ಆರು ಘಂಟೆಯಾಯಿತಂತೆ	**âru ghaṇṭe âyît' ante**
It is six o'clock, I am told	six bell it became it says
ಎರಡು ಘಂಟೆಯಿಂದ ಮೂರು ಘಂಟೇ ತನಕ	***y*eraḍu ghaṇṭeyinda mûru ghaṇṭê[1] tanaka**
From two to three o'clock	two from bell three of the bell till
ಹನ್ನೆರಡು ಘಂಟೆಯೊಳಗೆ ಬಾ	**hanneraḍu ghaṇṭey' oḷage bâ**
Come within twelve o'clock	twelve of the bell within come

27. ಯಾವ yâva=which?

ಯಾವನು yâvanu, ಯಾವಳು yâvaḷu (ಯಾವಾಕೆ yâvâke), ಯಾವದು yâvadu
=which man, woman, thing? (*G. welcher, welche, welches?*)

Remarks:—1. In the same way as the adjective yâva, other adjectives, relative participles (present, past and negative), and genitive cases of nouns are made pronouns by having the pronoun avanu, avaḷu, (or âtanu, âke), adu added to them, and may then be declined in the same way as these pronouns; *e. g.* čikkavanu, čikkavaḷu, čikkadu=a little one (person or thing).

---

[1] See Note 2 p. 38.

hôguvavanu, one who is going; hôdavanu=one who is gone; hogadavanu =one who does not go; ûrinavanu, ûrinavaḷu, ûrinadu=a person or thing of the village.

2. When adjective and genitive cases of nouns are to form the predicate of a sentence, they should always have the pronoun avanu, avaḷu etc. added to them; as, he is good, Kanarese, avanu *wo*ḷḷeyavanu, it is nice. Kan. adu čalôdu; he is of Dhârwar Kan. avanu Dhâravâḍad'avanu.

ಯಾವ ಕುದುರೆ ಚಲೋದು? *S.* (...ಒಳ್ಳೇದು? *C.*)	yâva kudure čalôdu? *S.* (...*wo*ḷlêdu? *C.*)
Which horse is the best?	which horse good?
ನಿಮಗೆ ಯಾವದು ಬೇಕು?	nimage yâvadu bêku?
Which do you want?	to you which is wanted
ಯಾವದನ್ನು (ಯಾವದು) ತಂದು ಕೊಡಲಿ?	yâvadannu (yâvadu)[1] tandu koḍali?
Which shall I bring you?	which h. brought let me give?
ನಿಮ್ಮಲ್ಲಿ ಯಾವನು ಹೋಗುತ್ತಾನೆ?	nimmalli yâvanu hôguttâne?
Which of you is going?	in you which man he goes?
ಯಾವನಿಗೆ ಹೋಗನ್ನುತ್ತೀರಿ?	yâvanige hôg'annuttîri?
Whom will you tell to go?	to which man go you say?
ಯಾವನನ್ನು (ಯಾವನ್ನ) ಕರಕೊಂಡು ಬರಲಿ?	yâvanannu (yâvanna) kara'koṇḍu barali?
Which of them shall I bring here?	which man h. called let me come?
ನೀವು ಯಾತರವರು? ನಾವು ಲಿಂಗವಂತರು	nivu yâtar'avaru[2]? nâvu liṅgavantaru
Of what caste are you? We are Lingaits	you of which they? we Lingaits
ಇದು ಯಾತರ ಹೂವು?	idu yâtara hûvu?
What kind of flower is this?	this of which flower?
ಯಾವಾಕೆ ನಿಮ್ಮಕ್ಕ? *S.* ಯಾವಳು...? *C.*	yâvâke nimm'akka? *S.* (yâvaḷu...? *C.*)
Which is your (elder) sister?	which woman your elder sister?
ಇವರೊಳಗೆ ಯಾವನ ಮೇಲೆ ಕಣ್ಣಿಟ್ಟಿ?	ivar'oḷage yâvana mêle kaṇṇ'iṭṭi[3]?
On which of these persons have you set your eyes?	their within on which man eye thou setst?

---

[1] The crude form *yâvadu* is more frequently used in the objective case than the accusative *yâvadannu*.

[2] About *yâtara* see note 1 p. 36; this phrase is commonly used when asking people's caste.

[3] *Iṭṭi* 2nd person, singular, past tense of *iḍu*, see No. 76.

28. ಯಾರು yâru = who (*G. wer*)?

Remarks:—Y â r u, instead of yâvaru, is the plural of y â v a n u and y â v a ḷ u (see No. 27), and it is incorrect to construe it with a verb in the singular; y â r û with a subsequent negative signifies *no one.*

ಇವರು ಯಾರು?	**ivaru yâru?**
Who are they? (who is this?)	these who?
ಯಾರವರು?	**yâr' avaru?**
Who is that? who is there?	who they?
ಯಾರು ಹೋಗುತ್ತಾರೆ? ಯಾರೂ ಇಲ್ಲ	**yâru hôguttâre? yâr'û illa**
Who will go? who is going? No one	who they go? who even is not
ಯಾರಾದರೂ ಹೋಗ ಬಹುದು	**yâr' âdar'û hôga bahudu**[1]
Any one may go	who if become even may go
ಬಂದವರ್ಯಾರು?	**band' avar' yâru?**
Who are the persons arrived?	they who came who?
ಯಾರನ್ನು ನೋಡಿದಿರಿ?	**yârannu nôḍidiri?**
Whom did you see?	whom you saw?
ಈ ಮಾತು ಯಾರಿಂದ ಕೇಳಿದಿರಿ?	**î mâtu yârinda kêḷidiri?**
From whom did you hear this matter?	this word from whom you heard?
ಯಾರಿಗೂ ಹೇಳಬೇಡ	**yârig'û hêḷa bêḍa**
Do not mention it to any one	to whom even to tell is not wanted
ಯಾರಿಗೂ ಹೇಳುವದಿಲ್ಲ	**yârigû hêḷuvad' illa**
I shan't tell any one	to whom even the saying is not
ಯಾರ ಕೈಯಲ್ಲಿತ್ತು?	**yâra keiyall' ittu?**
Who was in possession of this?	whose in hand it was?

29. ಏನು yênu = what (*G. was*)?

Remark:—*Y* ê n û with some negative following signifies *nothing.*

ಅದೇನು? *or* ಏನದು?	**ad'ênu?** *or* **yên'adu?**
What is that	that what? what that?
ಏನು ಕಳುಹಿಸಿದರು?	**yênu kaḷuhisidaru?**
What did they (he) send?	what they sent?

---

[1] About *yârâdarû* see note 1, p. 35; about *bahudu* s. note 5, p. 34.

ಏನೂ ಕಳುಹಿಸಲಿಲ್ಲ *or* ಏನೂ ಇಲ್ಲ	**yênû kaḷuhisal'illa,** *or* **yênû illa**
They did not send anything; nothing	what to send is not, what even is not
ಇದಕ್ಕೇನು ಕೊಡುತ್ತೀರಿ?	**idakk' ênu koḍuttîri?**
What will you give for this?	to this what you give?
ಏನೂ ಕೊಟ್ಟರೂ ನಾ ತಕ್ಕೊಳ್ಳುವದಿಲ್ಲ	**yênû koṭṭar'û nâ takkoḷḷuvad'illa**
Whatever you give I shall not take it	what even if given even I the taking is not
ಏನಾಯಿತು?	**yên' âyitu?**
What has happened? what is the matter? what has become of it what has been done?	what it became?
ಏನಾಯಿತೋ ಏನೋ?	**yên' âyit'ô yên'ô?**
I do not know what has happened, what the matter is, what has become of it, what has been done	what it became what?
ಅದೇನಂದರೆ	**ad' ên' andare** } *literally — if you*
That is to say; namely	that what if said } *say, "what is that?"*
ಅವನು ಹೇಳಿದ್ದೇನಂದರೆ	**avanu hêḷidd' ên' andare**
He said, etc.; what he said was this	he that which he said what if said
ಏನಾದರೂ ಮಾಡು	**yên' âdar'û mâḍu**
Do something; do whatever you [like	what if become even do

30. ಯಾತಕ್ಕೆ, ಯಾಕೆ yâtakke, yâke = why, wherefore (*G. warum*)?

ಯಾಕೆ ಬಂದಿರಿ? *or only* **ಯಾಕೆ?**	**yâke bandiri?** *or only* **yâke?**
Why are you come?	why you came? why?
ಯಾಕಿಲ್ಲ; ಹೀಗೆ ಬಂದೆವು	**yâk'illa; hîge bandevu**
For nothing particular	why not; thus we came
ಯಾಕೆ ಕೊಡಲಿಲ್ಲ? (-ಕೊಟ್ಟಿಲ್ಲ? *S.*)	**yâke koḍal' illa? (-koṭṭ'illa? *S.*)**
Why did you not give it (them)?	why to give is not? (h. given is not?)
ಇದೆಲ್ಲಾ ಯಾಕೆ?	**id'ellâ yâke?**
Why all this?	this all why?
ಮೂರು ಮಂದಿ ಯಾಕೆ? ಒಬ್ಬನೇ ಸಾಕು	**mûru mandi yâke? *w*obbanê sâku**[1]
Why three persons? one is enough	three persons why? *one* is enough

[1] See note 4 p. 34.

ಇಷ್ಟೆಲ್ಲಾ ಯಾತಕ್ಕೆ?	**isht̤'ellâ yâtakke?**
What is all this for? why all this [ado?	so much all wherefore?
ಇದು ಯಾತಕ್ಕೆ ಬೇಕು?	**idu yâtakke bêku?**
What is this for? why do you want [this?	this wherefore is wanted
ಯಾತಕ್ಕೆ ಬೇಕಂದಿರಾ (-ರೋ)?	**yâtakke bêk' andir'â (-rô)?**
Do you ask for what it is?	wherefore it is wanted you said?
ನಮಗೆ ಬೇಕಾಗಿಲ್ಲ, ಯಾಕಂದರೆ *etc.*	**namage bêk'âg'illa, yâk'andare**[1], *etc.*
We do not want it, for, *etc.*	to us it is wanted not, why if said
ಯಾಕೆ ಬಂದಿ? ಹೇಳು	**yâke bandi? hêḷu**
Why are you come? tell me	why thou camest? tell

31. ಹ್ಯಾಗೆ, ಹ್ಯಾಂಗೆ hyâge, hyâṅge = how (*G. wie*)?

ಇದು ಹ್ಯಾಗೆ *or* ಇದ್ಹ್ಯಾಗೆ?	**idu hyâge?** *or* **id'hyâge?**
How is this?	this how? this how?
ಹ್ಯಾಗೆ ಬಂದಿರಿ?	**hyâge bandiri?**
How did you come?	how you came?
ನಾವು ಬಂದದ್ದು ಹ್ಯಾಗಂದರೆ	**nâvu bandaddu hyâg'andare** } *lit. if you ask how?*
We came in this manner	we the h. come how if said
ಹ್ಯಾಗೆ ಬರೆದಿರಿ?	**hyâge barediri?**
How did you write?	how you wrote?
ಹ್ಯಾಗೆ ಬರೆಯ ಬೇಕಾಗಿತ್ತು?	**hyâge bareya bêkâg' ittu?**
How was it to be written?	how to write h. been wanted it was?
ಅದು ಹ್ಯಾಗಾದೀತು?	**adu hyâg'âdîtu?** (*See No. 10*)
How can that be?	that how it will become?
ಹ್ಯಾಗೂ ಕೊಡ ಬೇಕು	**hyâgû koḍa bêku**
You must give it anyhow	how even to give is wanted
ಹ್ಯಾಗಾದರೂ ಮಾಡ ಬೇಕು	**hyâg'âdarû mâḍa bêku**
It must by all means be done; ... be [made	how if become even to make is wanted
ಅದನ್ನು ಮಾಡುವದು ಹ್ಯಾಗೆ?	**adannu mâḍuvadu hyâge?**
How is it to be done? ... made?	that the making how?
ಹ್ಯಾಗಿರುತ್ತೀರಿ *or* ಹ್ಯಾಗಿದ್ಧೀರಿ?	**hyâg'iruttîri?** *or* **hyâg'iddhîri?**
How are you?	how you are? how you are?

[1] **Yâk'andare**, literally: "if you say (*or* ask) why" is commonly used with the meaning of the conjunction *for*, though Kanarese people avoid it as much as they can.

32. ಹೀಗೆ, ಹೀಂಗೆ **hîge, hiṅge** = thus, so, like this (*G. so wie dies*); ಹಾಗೆ, ಹಾಂಗೆ **hâge, hâṅge** = thus, so, like that (*G. so wie das*), also used as a postposition = like (*G. wie*).

ಹುಡುಗರು ಚಲೋ ಬರೆಯುವ ಹಾಗೆ ನೋಡಿರಿ	**huḍugaru čalô bareyuva hâge[1] nôḍiri**
See that the boys write well	**boys well writing like see**
ಹಾಗೆ ಬರೆಯ ಬಾರದು, ಹೀಗೆ ಬರೆಯಲಿ	**hâge bareya bâradu[2], hige bareyali**
Let them write like this, not like that	**like that to write it will not come, like this let them write**
ಇದರ ಹಾಗೆಯೇ ಬರೆಯಲಿ	**idara hâgeyê bareyali**
Let them write exactly like this	**of this like just let them write**
ಕೆಟ್ಟೋಗುವ ಹಾಗಿರುತ್ತಾನೆ; (... ಹಾಗಿದ್ದಾನೆ)	**keṭṭ'hôguva[3] hâg'iruttâne; (-hâg'iddhâne)**
He is likely to be corrupted (... ruined)	**being corrupted like he is**
ಅವ ಕೆಡದ ಹಾಗೆ ಏನು ಮಾಡುತ್ತೀ?	**ava keḍada hâge *y*ênu mâḍutti?**
What will you do lest he be corrupted (... ruined)?	**he in order not to become bad what thou doest?**
ಏನೂ ಮಾಡುವ ಹಾಗಿಲ್ಲ	***y*ênû mâḍuva hâg'illa**
There is nothing to be done	**what even doing like is not**
ತಂದೆಯ ಹಾಗೆ ಮಗನು	**tandeya hâge maganu**
The son is like the father	**father's like son**
ಹಾಗಾದರೆ ಬಿಡಿರಿ	**hâg'âdare biḍiri**
Then give it up	**thus if become leave**
ಹೀಗಿರಲಿಕ್ಕೆ *or* ಹೀಗಿರಲಿಕ್ಕಾಗಿ	**hig'iralikke *or* hig' íralikk'âgi**
This being the case; therefore	**thus to be, thus to be h. become**
ಹೀಗಿರುವಲ್ಲಿ *or* ಹೀಗಿರುವದರಿಂದ	**hig' iruv' alli *or* hig' iruvadarinda[4]**
This being the case; for this reason	**thus being there, thus from the being**

[1] The word *hâge* is frequently joined to the relative present, past, and negative participles to form adverbial phrases expressing manner or object. To understand these phrases it should be remembered that *hâge* is properly a noun signifying "manner" or "object"; *bareyuva hâge* signifies "the writing manner" or the "writing object", *i.e.* the manner of writing, or the object of writing, and also "in the manner" or "with the object of writing".

[2] *Bâradu*, see note 5, p. 35.

[3] *Keṭṭ'hôgu* = *keṭṭu* + *hôgu*. *Keṭṭu* is the verbal p. p. of *keḍu*. In composition with *hôgu* it forms a new verb, signifying—to go bad, to be corrupted, to go to ruin.

[4] The verbal noun *iruvadu* is declined like the pronoun *adu*.

33. ಎಷ್ಟು *yeshṭu* = how much, how many? ಇಷ್ಟು **ishṭu** = this much, so much, so many; ಅಷ್ಟು **ashṭu** = that much, so much, so many; ಅಷ್ಟೂ, ಅಷ್ಟರೂ **ashṭû, ashṭarû** = all, the whole (*G. wie viel? so viel, alle, alles*).

ಎಷ್ಟು ಮಂದಿ ಹೋದರು?	*yeshṭu* **mandi hôdaru?**
How many persons have gone? ... [went?	**how many people went?**
ಅಷ್ಟರೂ ಹೋದರು	**ashṭar'û**[1] **hôdaru**
They have all gone	**all even they went** [**kaḷ'eshṭu?**
ನಿಮಗೆಷ್ಟು ಮಕ್ಕಳು *or* ನಿಮಗೆ ಮಕ್ಕಳೆಷ್ಟು?	**nimag'eshṭu makkaḷu? nimage mak-**
How many children have you?	**to you how many children? to you children how many?**
ನಿಮಗಿರುವಷ್ಟು ಮಂದಿ	**nimag'iruv' ashṭu mandi**
As many as you have	**to you being as much people**
ಎಷ್ಟೊತ್ತಾಯಿತು?	*yesht'* **hott' âyitu?**
What is the time?	**how much time it became?**
ಅಷ್ಟು ಬಹಳ ಹೊತ್ತಾಗಲಿಲ್ಲ	**ashṭu bahaḷa hott' âgal' illa**
It is not so very late	**so much much time to become is not**
ಎಷ್ಟಕ್ಕೆ ಕೊಡುತ್ತೀ?	*yeshṭakke* **koḍutti?**
For how much will you give it?	**to how much thou givest?**
ನೀವು ಕೊಡುವಷ್ಟು ತಕ್ಕೊಳ್ಳುತ್ತೇನೆ	**nîvu koḍuv' ashṭu takkoḷḷuttêne**
I shall take as much as you give	**you which give as much I take**
ಎಷ್ಟು ಕರದರೂ ಬರುವದಿಲ್ಲ	*yeshṭu* **karadar'û baruvad'illa**
He won't come though he has often been called	**how much if called even the coming is not**
ಎಷ್ಟು ಹೇಳಿದರೂ ಕೇಳುವದಿಲ್ಲ	*yeshṭu* **hêḷidar'û kêḷuvad'illa**
Whatever I tell him, he won't listen (obey)	**how much if said even the hearing is not**

34. *The same continued.*

ಒಂದಿಷ್ಟು *wondishṭu* = a little, ಎರಡಷ್ಟು *yeraḍashṭu* = twice as much

ಇದನ್ನು ಮಾಡಲಿಕ್ಕೆ ನಾವೆಷ್ಟರವರು?	**idannu mâḍalikke nâv'eshṭar' avaru?**
Who are we that we should do this?	**this to do we of how much they?**

[1] The termination "a r û gives the word a personal meaning to the effect that it signifies "all persons", *û* is the conjunctive particle signifying "even, also, and".

ಈ ಕೆಲಸ ಎಷ್ಟರಲ್ಲಿ ಆಗ ಬಹುದು? — î kelasa *y*eshṭāralli âga bahudu?
Within what sum may this job be done? — this work in how much to be done it can?

ಅಷ್ಟು ಬೇಡ, ಇಷ್ಟೇ ಸಾಕು — ashṭu bêḍa, ishṭê sâku
Not so much as that, this much [will do — that much is not wanted, *this much* is enough

ಬೇಕಾದಷ್ಟು ಕೊಡುತ್ತೇನೆ — bêk'âd' ashṭu koḍuttêne
I shall give you as much as you [want — as much as was wanted I give

ನಿಮಗಿದ್ದಷ್ಟು ಕೊಡಿರಿ — nimag' idd'ashṭu koḍiri
Give as much as you have; give [all you have — to you as much as was give

ಇನ್ನೂ ಎರಡಷ್ಟು ಅದೆ (...ಉಂಟು) — innû *y*eraḍashṭu ade (...unṭu)
There is still twice as much as this — yet even twice as much is (is)

ನಾವು ಬರುವಷ್ಟರೊಳಗೆ (-ರಲ್ಲಿ) ಹೋದರು — nâvu baruv'ashṭar'oḷage(-ralli) hôdaru
They went away before we arrived — within that much which we came they went

ಒಂದಿಷ್ಟು ಕೂಡ್ರಿ (ಕೂಡ್ರಿರಿ) — *w*ond'ishṭu kûḍri (kûḍriri)
Sit down a little — a little sit down

ಸ್ವಲ್ಪ ಕೂತುಕೊಳ್ಳಿರಿ — svalpa kûtukoḷḷiri[1]
Sit down a little — a little sit down

ಈ ಹುಡುಗರಿಗೆ ಒಂದಿಷ್ಟು (ಸ್ವಲ್ಪ) ನೋಡಿರಿ — î huḍugarige *w*ond'ishṭu (svalpa) [nôḍiri
Look after these boys a little — these to boys a little (a little) look

35. *The same continued.*

ನಮ್ಮ ಕಷ್ಟ ಇಷ್ಟೇ ಅಲ್ಲ — namma kashṭa ishṭ'ê alla
Our trouble is not a little only — our trouble *this much* not

ತಕ್ಕೊಂಡು ಬಂದದ್ದೆಲ್ಲಾ ಇಷ್ಟೇ? — takkoṇḍu bandadd'ellâ ishṭ'ê?
Is this all you (*a. p.*) have brought? — that which is brought all this much?

ಇಷ್ಟೇ ಸೈ — ishṭ'ê sei
Yes, this is all — *this much* right

ಇನ್ನಷ್ಟು ಓದು — inn' ashṭu *w*ôdu
Read a little more — yet that much read

[1] *Kûtu* is rel. p. p. of *kûḍru, kûtukoḷḷu* = to sit down. Only the latter half of this compound is conjugated.

ತನ್ನಿಂದಾದಷ್ಟು ಓದಿದ	tannind' âd' ashṭu *w*ôdida
He read as much as he could	by himself which is done that much he read
ಆದಷ್ಟು ಕಳುಹಿಸು	âd' ashṭu kaḷuhisu
Send as much as is finished; ...as much as you can	that much which was done send
ನೀವಷ್ಟರೂ ಬರ ಬೇಡಿರಿ	nîv'ashṭar'û bara bêḍiri
Don't come all of you	you all even to come you are not wanted
ನಾ ಹೇಳಿದಷ್ಟೇ ಮಂದಿ ಬರಲಿ	nâ hêḷid' ashṭê mandi barali
Let only so many come as I said	which I said *so many* people let come
ಇಷ್ಟೇ ಮಂದಿಯಿಂದಾದೀತೇ?	ishṭê mandiyind' âdîtê?
Can it be done by so many people only?	*so many* by people it will be done?
ಆಗ ಬಹುದು	âga bahudu
Yes, it may be done	to be done it will come

36. ಆಗ, ಆಗಲು âga, âgalu = that time, then; ಆಗ್ಯೆ âgye = then (*G. dann*); ಈಗ, ಈಗಲು îga, îgalu = this time, now; ಈಗ್ಯೆ îgye = now (*G. jetzt*); ಯಾವಾಗ yâvâga = when (*G. wann?*); ಯಾವಾಗಲೂ yâvâgalû = always (*G. immer*)

ಯಾವಾಗ ಎದ್ದಿರಿ?	yâvâga *y*eddiri[1]?
When did you get up?	when you rose?
ಆಗಲೇ ಎದ್ದೆವು	âgalê *y*êddevu
We got up some time ago	just then we rose
ಈಗ ಏಳುತ್ತೇವೆ	îga *y*êḷuttêve
We shall get up presently	now we rise
ಯಾವಾಗ ಊರಿಗೆ ಹೋಗುತ್ತೀರಿ?	yâvâga ûrige hôguttîri?
When are you going abroad? (*G. über Feld*)	when to town you go?
ಯಾವಾಗಾದರೂ (...ಗಲಾದರೂ *C.*) ಹೋಗುತ್ತೇವೆ	yâvâg'âdar'û (-gal'âdar'û) hôgut-têve
We (I) go now and then	when if done even we go
ಯಾವಾಗಲೂ ಮನೆಯಲ್ಲಿರ ಬೇಡ	yâvâgalû maneyall' ira bêḍa
Do not stay always at home	always in the house to be is not wanted

[1] *Yeddu* verb, p. p. of *yêḷu*, to rise.

ಆಗ್ಯಾಗ್ಯೆ ನಮ್ಮ ಮನೆಗೆ ಬರುತ್ತಾ ಇರು	**âgy'âgye namma manege baruttà iru**
Come to my house now and then	then them our to house coming be
ಇವರನ್ನು ನೋಡುವಾಗ ಕಣ್ಣೀರು ಬರುತ್ತವೆ	**ivarannu nôḍuvâga kaṇ'nîru baru-ttave**[1]
When I see them shed tears	these seeing then eye-water come
ನಾವು ಕರದಾಗ ಯಾರೂ ಬರಲಿಲ್ಲ	**nâvu karad' âga**[2] **yârû baral' illa**
No one came when we (I) called	which we called then who even to come is not
ಅವರು ಬಂದಾಗ ಕೊಡಿರಿ	**avaru band'âga**[2] **koḍiri**
Give it them when they come	which they come then give

37. ಎಂದು **yendu**=when? ಅಂದು **andu**=then; ಇಂದು **indu**=now, to-day (*G. wann?—dann,—jetzt, heute*).

Yendû *or* **yendigû** (Dative) with a subsequent negation signifies *never*.

ಎಂದು ಮನೆಗೆ ಬಂದಿರಿ?	**yendu manege bandiri?**
When did you come home?	when to house you came?
ಇಂದು ಬಂದೆವು	**indu bandevu**
We (I) came to-day [ವಾಯಿತು)	to day we came [âyi-tu)
ಇಂದಿಗೆ ಮೂರು ದಿವಸಾಯಿತು (ದಿವಸ	**indige mûru divas'âyitu divasa-v-**
Three days ago	to this day three day it became
ಅವರ ಮನೆಗೆ ಎಂದೂ ಹೋಗಿದ್ದಿಲ್ಲ (ಹೋಗಲಿಲ್ಲ *C.*)	**avara manege yendû hôg'idd'illa**[3] (**hôgal'illa** *C.*)
I (*a. p.*) have never been to their (his) house	their to house never h gone h. been is not (to go is not)
ಇಂಥಾ ಕೆಲಸ ಎಂದಿಗೂ ಮಾಡಲಿಕ್ಕಿಲ್ಲ	**inthâ kelasa yendigû mâḍalikk'illa**
I (*a. p.*) shall never do such a thing as this	such work never to do is not
ಎಂದಾದರೂ ಇಂಥಾದ್ದನ್ನು ಕಂಡಿರಾ (-ರೋ)?	**yend'âdar'û inthâddannu kaṇḍirâ (-rô)?**
Did you ever see any thing like this?	when if done even such a thing you [saw?
ಎಂದೂ ಕಂಡಿದ್ದಿಲ್ಲ (ಕಾಣಲಿಲ್ಲ *C.*)	**yendû kaṇḍ'idd'illa**[3] (**kâṇal'illa** *C.*)
I never saw it	never h. seen h. been not (to see is not)

---

1 Nîru is generally constructed with the verb in the plural.

2 Nâvu karada + âga = that time at which we called. Avaru banda + âga = that time at which they came.

3 *Hôg'*=*hôgi*, *idd,*=*iddu*, *kaṇḍ'*=*kaṇḍu* are verbal past participles.

ಅಂದಿನಿಂದ ಅವನನ್ನು (ಅವನ್ನ) ನೋಡಲಿಲ್ಲ andininda avanannu (avanna) nôḍal'illa
I have not seen him since that day from then him to see is not

ಇವನು ಚಿಕ್ಕಂದಿನಿಂದ ಕೆಟ್ಟವನೇ ivanu čikk'andininda[1] keṭṭ'avanê[2]
He has been wicked from his childhood he from childhood bad *he*

ಇಂದಿನಿಂದ ಹತ್ತು ದಿವಸದ ತನಕ indininda hattu divasada tanaka
For ten days from to-day from to-day ten of day till

38. ನೋಡು nôḍu = to look, to see *(G. sehen.)*

Conjugation of the **Regular** Verb ending in u.

1. From the *crude form* **nôḍu**, the Imperative and Negative moods are formed; see No. 1 and No. 13.
2. From the *pres. verb. part.* **nôdutta**, the present tense is formed; see No. 1.
3. From the *pr. & fut. rel. p.* **nôḍuva**, the 2nd Future tense is formed; see below
4. From the *past rel. part.* **nôḍida**, the Past tense is formed; see No. 2.
5. „ „ „ **nôḍida**, after dropping the termination da the 1st Future is formed; see No. 10.

2nd Future Tense.

Singular:	*Plural:*
nôḍuv-enu, I shall see	**nôḍuv-evu**, we shall see
nôḍuv-i, thou wilt „	**nôḍuv-iri**, you will „
nôḍuv-anu, he will „	**nôḍuv-aru**, they *(m. & f.)* will see
nôḍuv-aḷu, she „ „	
nôḍuv-adu, it „ „	**nôḍuv-avu**, they *(n.)* will see

Remark:—The Second future asserts with certainty, whereas the First future asserts somewhat doubtfully.

ಈ ಹುಡುಗರಿಗೆ ಯಾರು ನೋಡುತ್ತಾರೆ? î hudugarige yâru nôḍuttâre?
Who looks after these boys? these to boys who they look?

ಆಕೆ (ಅವಳು *C.*) ನೋಡುತ್ತಾಳೆ âke (avaḷu *C.*) nôḍuttâḷe
She looks (after them) she she looks

ಯಾರೂ ನೋಡುವದಿಲ್ಲ yârû nôḍuvad' illa
No one looks (after them); nobody sees it who even the looking is not

---

[1] As in many other similar combinations the adjective *čikka* qualifies the noun *andu* meaning, "the time of being little childhood".

[2] *Keṭṭa*, relative p. p. of *keḍu*, see Rem. 1, No. 27.

ನೋಡುವವರಿಲ್ಲ	nôḍuv' avar'illa
There is none to look	seeing ones are not
ಈ ಕೆಲಸ ನಮ್ಮಪ್ಪ ನೋಡುತ್ತಾನೆ	î kelasa namm'appa nôḍuttâne
My fahther will do this job	this work our father sees
ಇನ್ನೂ ಕೆಲವು ದಿವಸ ನೋಡ ಬೇಕು	innû kelavu divasa nôḍa bêku
He (*a. p.*) must do it a few days more: we (*a. p.*) must wait a few days longer	yet even some day to see is wanted
ನೋಡಿ ಓದ ಬೇಕು	nôdi *w*ôda bêku
You (*a. p.*) should read carefully	h. seen to read is wanted
ಆ ಊರು (ಊರನ್ನು) ನೋಡಿದವರ್ಯಾರು?	â ûru (ûrannu) nôḍid'avar' yâru?[1]
Who has seen that town?	that town (town *acc.*) they who saw who?
ನಾವು ನೋಡಿದೆವು	nâvu nôḍidevu
We saw it; we have seen it	we saw
ನೋಡದವರು ಬಹಳ ಮಂದಿ	nôḍad' avaru bahaḷa mandi
There are many who have not seen it (*a. p.*)	they who did not see many people

39. *The same continued.*

ಅವನನ್ನು (ಅವನ್ನ) ಕಂಡರೆ, ಕರಕೊಂಡು ಬಾ	avanannu (avanna) kaṇḍare kara-koṇḍu bâ
If you see him, bring him here	him if seen, h. called come
ಆತನನ್ನು (ಆತನ್ನ) ಕಂಡೇನು	âtanannu (âtanna) kaṇḍênu
I may see him, I shall probably see him	him (*hon.*) I may see
ಕಾಣದಿದ್ದರೆ, ಏನು ಮಾಡಲಿ?	kâṇad' iddare, *y*ênu mâḍali?
What shall I (*a. p.*) do, if I should not see him (*a. p.*)?	not h. seen if been what let (*a.p.*) do?
ನೋಡಲಿಯೋ (-ಯಾ)?	nôḍali-y-ô (-y-â)?
Shall I see?	let see?
ನೋಡೋಣ, ಬಾ *S.* ನೋಡುವ, ಬಾ *C.*	nôḍôṇa, bâ *S.*, nôḍuva bâ *C.*
Come, let us see	let us see, come; let us see, come
ನೀನು ಅಲ್ಲಿ ನೋಡಿದ್ದೇನು?	nînu alli nôḍidd' ênu?
What did you see there?	thou there the having seen what?

[1] See Rem. 1, No. 27.

ನಮ್ಮನ್ನು ನೋಡ ಬಾ — nammannu nôḍa bâ

Come to see us (me) — us to see come

ನಿಮ್ಮನ್ನು ನೋಡಲಿಕ್ಕೆ (ನೋಡುವದಕ್ಕೆ) ಬಂದಿದ್ಧೇನೆ — nimmannu nôḍalikke (nôḍuvadakke[1]) band'iddhêne

I am come to see you — you to see (to the seeing) h. come I am

ಈ ಕುದುರೆ ಏನು ನೋಡುತ್ತದೆ? — î kudure yênu nôḍuttade?

What is the horse seeing? (...looking at?) — this horse what it sees?

ಎರಡನೇ ಕುದುರೆಯನ್ನು ನೋಡಿತು — yeraḍanê kudureyannu nôḍitu

It saw another horse — second horse it saw

40. ಕರೆ kare = to call (*G. rufen*). See conjugation of the Regular Verb ending in e (or i.) No. 18.

ಉಣ್ಣಲಿಕ್ಕೆ ಮಂದೀ ಕರೆಯ ಬೇಕು — uṇṇalikke mandî[2] kareya bêku

You should invite people to dinner — to eat people to call is wanted

ಅಷ್ಟರನ್ನು ಕರೆದೆ(ನು) — ashṭarannu karede(nu)

I have invited all of them — all I called

ನಿಮ್ಮಕ್ಕನ(ನ್ನು) ಕರೆ — nimm'[3]akkana(nnu) kare

Call (invite) your (elder) sister — your elder sister (*acc.*) call

ಆಕೆಯನ್ನು ಕರೆಯುತ್ತೇನೆ — âkeyannu kareyuttêne

I shall call (invite) her — her I call

ನಿಮ್ಮಪ್ಪ ಇಲ್ಲ, ಕರೇ ಕಳುಹಿಸು — nimm'appa[3] illa, karê[4] kaḷuhisu

Your father is not here, send for him — your father is not, to call send

ಆತನನ್ನು ಕರೆಸುತ್ತೇನೆ — âtanannu karesuttêne[5]

I shall send for him — him (*hon.*) I cause to call

ಅವನಿಗೆ ಕರೆಯುವದು ಯಾಕೆ? — avanige kareyuvadu yâke?

Why call him? — to him the calling why?

ಕರೆಯದಿದ್ದರೆ ಚೆಲೋದು *S.* (-ಒಳ್ಳೇದು *C.*) — kareyad'iddare čalôdu *S.* (woḷḷêdu *C.*)

It is better not to call him — not h. called if been nice (good)

---

[1] *Nôḍuvadakke* is dative case of the present verbal noun *nôḍuvadu* which follows the pronoun *adu* in its mode of declension.

[2] *Mandî*, instead of *mandiyannu*, a form of the accusative case in which the terminal vowel is lengthened.

[3] It is considered abusive language to say even to a little child: "*ninna akka, ninna appa, ninna tangi*", *etc.*; in fact, these combinations are frequently used by Hindus to abuse one another, especially the expression "*ninna henḍati*=thy wife".

[4] Instead of *kareya*.

[5] See Note 4, p. 30.

ಅವನಿಗೆ ಕರೆದು ಉಣ್ಣಲಿಕ್ಕೆ ಕೊಡು	avanige karedu uṇṇalikke koḍu
Call him and give him something to eat	him h. called to eat give
ಇವರನ್ನು ಕರಕೊಂಡು ಹೋಗು	ivarannu kara koṇḍu hôgu
Take these persons away; accompany them	these (*acc.*) h. called h. taken go

41. ಕಾಣು kâṇu = to see, to appear, to seem

(*G. sehen, erscheinen, scheinen*).

Conjugation of Irregular Verbs.

The conjugation of kâṇu and other irregular verbs follows that of regular verbs, it is only required to know the following forms:—the past verbal and relative participles, the 3rd person singular neuter of the past tense, and, in a few cases, the 2nd person of the imperative mood, when all the other verbal forms may be formed as shown in No. 38. Of the verbs on pp. 6 and 7 the following are irregular:

Crude Form	Past Verbal Participle	Past Relative Participle	3rd Person Sing. Neuter of the Past Tense	2nd Person Imperative where irregular
iru	iddu	idda	ittu	
baru	bandu	banda	bantu	bâ, *pl.* barri *or* banni
taru	tandu	tanda	tantu	tâ, *pl.* tarri *or* tanni
âgu	âgi	âda	âyitu	
hôgu	hôgi	hôda	hôyitu	
kâṇu	kaṇḍu	kaṇḍa	kaṇḍitu	
yêḷu	yeddu	yedda	yedditu	
bîḷu	biddu	bidda	bittu	
koḍu	koṭṭu	koṭṭa	koṭṭitu	
keḍu	keṭṭu	keṭṭa	keṭṭitu	
biḍu	biṭṭu	biṭṭa	biṭṭitu	
iḍu	iṭṭu	iṭṭa	iṭṭitu	
annu	andu	anda	anditu	
nillu	nintu *or* nindu	ninta *or* ninda	nintitu	
koḷḷu	koṇḍu	koṇḍa	koṇḍitu	
kûḍru	kûtu	kûta	kûtitu	

ಅವನ ಕಣ್ಣು ಕಾಣುವದಿಲ್ಲ	avana kaṇṇu kâṇuvad' illa
He cannot see; he is blind	his eyes the seeing is not
ಹಾಗೆ ಕಾಣುತ್ತದೆ	hâge kâṇuttade
So it seems (...appears)	like that it appears
ಅವನನ್ನು (ಅವನ್ನ) ಕಂಡಿಯಾ? [him?	avanannu (avanna) kaṇḍi-y-â?
Did you see him? Have you seen	him thou sawst?
ಕಂಡ ಹಾಗಾಯಿತು	kaṇḍa hâg'âyitu
It is as if I had seen him; I have as much as seen him	seen so it became
ಕುದುರೆ ಕಂಡುಕೊಂಡರೋ? C. (...ಕೊಂಡರೇನು? S.)	kudure kaṇḍukoṇḍar'ô? C. (-koṇḍar'ênu? S.) [what?)
Has the horse been found?	horse h. seen they took? (they took
ಕಂಡುಕೊಳ್ಳಲಿಲ್ಲ C. (ಕಂಡುಕೊಂಡಿಲ್ಲ S.)	kaṇḍukoḷḷal' illa, (kaṇḍukoṇḍ' illa)
No, it has not been found	h. seen to take is not, h. seen h. taken is not
ಅದು ಕಾಣದೆ ಹೋಯಿತು [to be seen	adu kâṇade hôyitu
It has disappeared; it is nowhere	that not h. appeared it went
ಕಂಡರೆ ನಮಗೆ ಹೇಳು	kaṇḍare namage hêḷu
If you see it, tell me	if seen to us tell
ಕಾಣಲಿಕ್ಕಿಲ್ಲ	kâṇalikk' illa
It will probably not be found; ...not be seen	to appear is not
ಕಂಡವರ ಮನೆಗೆ ಹೋಗ ಬೇಡ	kaṇḍ' avara manege hôga bêḍa
Do not visit every one indiscriminately	of those whom you saw to house to go is not wanted

42. ಅವಳು avaḷu = she (*Remote*); ಇವಳು ivaḷu = she (*near*); ಆಕೆ âke = she (*rem.*), ಈಕೆ îke = she (*near*), the latter two honorary (*G. sie; jene, diese*)

See Note 1, p. 5.

ಈಕೆ ಯಾರ ಹೆಂಡತಿ? S. (ಇವಳು...? C.)	îke yâra heṇḍati? S. (ivaḷu...? C.)
Whose wife is she?	she whose wife? (she...?)
ಈಕೆ ನಮ್ಮಣ್ಣನ ಹೆಂಡತಿ S. (ಇವಳು... C.)	îke namm' aṇṇana heṇḍati S. (ivaḷu...C.)
She is my elder brother's wife	she our elder brother's wife (she...)

ಈಕೆಯ ಅಕ್ಕ ಬಹಳ ಒಳ್ಳ್ಯಾಕೆ *S.* (ಇವಳ...ಒಳ್ಳೆಯವಳು *C.*)	**îkeya akka bahaḷa** ***wo*****ḷḷ-y-âke**[1] *S.* (**ivaḷa ...*****wo*****ḷḷe-y-avaḷu** *C.*)
Her elder sister is a very good woman	her elder sister very good she
ಆಕೆಗೆ ಚಿಕ್ಕ ಮಗಳಿರುತ್ತಾಳೆ (ಅವಳಿಗೆ...)	**âkege čikka magaḷ' iruttâḷe** (**avaḷige...**)
She has got a little daughter	to her little daughter she is
ಆಕೆಯನ್ನು ಕಂಡಿರೇನು? *S.* (ಅವಳನ್ನು ಕಂಡಿರೋ? *C.*)	**âkeyannu kaṇḍir'ênu?** *S.*(**avaḷannu kaṇḍirô?** *C.*)
Have you seen her?	her you saw what? (her you saw?)
ಇವರು ನಿಮ್ಮ ತಾಯಿಯವರಲ್ಲಾ?	**ivaru nimma tâyiy' avar' allâ?**[2]
This is your mother, is she not?	they your mother's they not so?
ಯಾವಾಕೆ ನಿಮ್ಮಕ್ಕ? *S.*(ಯಾವಳು...?*C.*)	***y*****âv'âke nimm' akka?** *S.* (**yâvaḷu ...?** *C.*)
Which is your elder sister?	which she your elder sister?
ಆಕೆಯು ನಮ್ಮಕ್ಕ *S.* (ಅವಳು...*C.*)	**âkeyu**[3]**namm' akka** *S.* (**avaḷu...** *C.*)
That is my elder sister	she our elder sister
ಈಕೆಯು ನಮ್ಮ ತಂಗಿ *S.* (ಇವಳು...*C.*)	**îkeyu**[3] **namma taṅgi** *S.* (**ivaḷu...** *C.*)
This is my younger sister	she our younger sister
ಈ ಚಿಕ್ಕಾಕೆ ನನ್ನ ಮಗಳು	**î čikk' âke nanna magaḷu**
This little girl is my daughter	this little she my daughter

43. ತಾನು **tânu**=**himself, herself,** itself *(G. er, sie, es, selbst; pl. Sie).*

ಎಲ್ಲಾ ತಾನೇ ಯಾಕೆ ಮಾಡಿದ?	***y*****ellâ tânê yâke mâḍida?**
Why did he everything himself?	all *himself* why he did?
ತಾನು ಮಾಡುತ್ತೇನೆಂತ ಹೇಳಿದ	**tânu mâḍuttên' enta**[4] **hêḷida**
He said he would do (make) it	himself I do saying he said
ಎಲ್ಲಾ ತನ್ನ ಮೇಲೆ ತಕ್ಕೊಂಡ	***y*****ellâ tanna mêle takkoṇḍa**
He took it all upon himself	all on himself he took
ತನ್ನ ಮಕ್ಕಳಿಗೆ ಕೊಡದೆ ತಾನೇ ಉಂಡಳು	**tanna makkaḷige koḍade tânê uṇḍaḷu**
She ate (it) herself without giving anything to her children	her own to children not h. given herself she ate

---

1 For *wollêy'âke.*

2 In polite language the pronoun *avaru* is often added to the words *appa, tâyi, aṇṇa, taṅgi,* etc.

3 Nominative case, instead of which the crude form is generally used in conversation.

4 *Enta=ennutta,* present verbal participle of *yennu=annu,* I say; or *yendu* past v. p. of *yennu,* is always added after a quotation before the verb *hêḷu* or another verb of a similar meaning; only before the word *annu* it is generally omitted.

ತನಗೆ ಬೇಕಂದಳು	**tanage bêk' andaḷu**
She said she wanted it herself (*with the accent on* "tanage"); She said she wanted it (*with the accent on* "bêku")	to herself it is wanted she said
ತಮ್ಮ ಮಕ್ಕಳನ್ನು ಕರಕೊಂಡು ಬಂದರೋ?	**tamma makkaḷannu karakoṇḍu [bandar'ô?**
Have they brought their children along with them?	their children h. called they came?
ತಮಗೆ ಮಕ್ಕಳಿಲ್ಲನ್ನುತ್ತಾರೆ	**tamage makkaḷ' ill' annuttâre**
They say they have no children	to themselves children are not they say
ತಮ್ಮ ಬರೋಣ ಯಾವಾಗಾಯಿತು?	**tamma[1] barôṇa[2] yâvâg' âyitu?**
When did you arrive?	their the arriving when it happened?
ತಮಗೇನು ತರಬೇಕು?	**tamag' ênu tara bêku?**
What shall I bring you?	to themselves what to bring is wanted?
ತಮ್ಮ ಕುದುರೆ ಆಗಲೇ ಬಂತು	**tamma kudure âgalê bantu**
Your horse is already come	of themselves horse *then* it came

44. ಮಂದಿ **mandi** = people, persons (*G. Leute, Personen*); only used for more than one person.

ನಿಮ್ಮ ಮನೆಯಲ್ಲಿ ಎಷ್ಟು ಮಂದಿ ಇರುತ್ತಾರೆ?	**nimma maneyalli yeshṭu mandi iruttâre?**
How many persons are in your house?	your in the house how many people they are?
ಮೂರೇ ಮಂದಿ	**mûrê mandi**
Only three	*three* people
ಬಹಳ ಮಂದಿ ಇರುತ್ತಾರೆ	**bahaḷa mandi iruttâre**
There are many people	many people they are
ನಿಮ್ಮ ತಮ್ಮ ಎಲ್ಲಿ?	**nimma tamma yelli?**
Where is your younger brother?	your younger brother where?
ಮಂದಿ(ಯನ್ನು) ಕರೆಯಲಿಕ್ಕೆ ಹೋದ	**mandi (yannu) kareyalikke hôda**
He has gone to call people; ... to invite guests	people to call he went

---

[1] *Tâvu* is used in polite language, when speaking to a superior, like the German *Sie*.

[2] *Barôṇa*, a verbal noun, the same as *baruvadu*. The phrase *barôṇavâyitu*, present tense, *barôṇavâguttade*, which may be used for any person, is likewise used in courteous language.

ಅಷ್ಟು ಮಂದಿಗೆ ಉಣ್ಣಲಿಕ್ಕೆ ಹೇಳ ಬೇಡ	**ashṭu mandige uṇṇalikke hêḷa bêḍa**
Do not invite so many people to dinner	so many to people to eat to say is not wanted
ಮಂದಿಯ ಮಾತು ಕೇಳ ಬೇಡ	**mandiya mâtu kêḷa bêḍa**
Do not listen to what people say	of people word to hear is not wanted
ನಾಲ್ಕು ಮಂದಿ ಹೇಳಿದ ಹಾಗೆ ಮಾಡು	**nâlku mandi hêḷida hâge mâḍu**
Follow the advice of society	four people said so do
ಇವರು ಕೆಟ್ಟ ಮಂದಿ	**ivaru keṭṭa[1] mandi**
These are bad people	these become bad people
ಇವರು ನಮ್ಮ ಮಂದಿಯ ಹಾಗಲ್ಲ	**ivaru namma mandiya hâg'alla**
They are not like our people	these our people's like not

45. ಬಿಡು **biḍu**=to leave, forsake, give up (*G. lassen, fahren lassen*). See No. 41.

ಈ ಮನೆ ಬಿಡ ಬೇಕು (ಬಿಡಲಿಕ್ಕೇ ...)	**î mane biḍa bêku (biḍalikkê ...)**
You (*a. p.*) should leave this house	this house to leave is wanted
ಬಿಡದಿದ್ದರೆ ನಿಮ್ಮನ್ನು ಹೊರಗೆ ಹಾಕಿಸುತ್ತೇವೆ	**biḍad'iddare nimmannu horage hâkisuttêve**
If you don't leave it, I shall have you turned out	not h. left if been you out we cause to throw
ನನ್ನ ಕೈಬಿಡುತ್ತೀರೋ? (ಬಿಡುತ್ತೀರೇನು?)	**nanna kei biḍuttîrô? (biḍuttîr' ênu?)**
Will you forsake me? are you going to ...?	me you leave? (you leave what?)
ನಿನ್ನ(ನ್ನು) ಬಿಡುವದಿಲ್ಲ	**ninna(nnu) biḍuvad' illa**
I shall not forsake you	thee the forsaking is not
ಈ ಕೆಲಸ ಬಿಟ್ಟು ಕೊಟ್ಟೆ	**î kelasa biṭṭu koṭṭe**
I have given up this business; ... job	this work h. given up I gave
ಹೌದು, ಎಲ್ಲಾ ಕೆಡಿಸಿ ಬಿಟ್ಟಿ	**houdu, yellâ keḍisi[2] biṭṭi**
Yes, you have spoilt (ruined) every [thing	yes, all h. spoilt thou leftst
ಅನ್ನಾ ಎಲ್ಲಿಟ್ಟುಕೊಂಡರು?	**annâ yell' iṭṭukoṇḍaru[3]?**
Where is the rice kept?	rice where they kept?

---

[1] See note 2, p. 49.

[2] *Keḍu*=to become bad, *keḍisu*=to make bad, to spoil, to ruin,

[3] *Iṭṭukoḷḷu* (see No. 17)=to keep.

ಎಲ್ಲಾ ಉಂಡು ಬಿಟ್ಟರು	**yellâ uṇḍu biṭṭaru**
It is all eaten	all h. eaten they left
ಬೆಂಕಿಯಲ್ಲಿ ಹಾಕಿ ಬಿಟ್ಟರು	**beṅkiyalli hâki biṭṭaru**
It has been thrown into the fire	in the fire h. thrown they left
ಎಷ್ಟು ಕಷ್ಟ ಬಿಡುತ್ತಾರೆ!	**yeshṭu kashṭa biḍuttâre**[1]!
What a deal of trouble they take!	how much trouble they leave (put forth)!

46. ಕಣ್ಣು **kaṇṇu** = eye (*G. Auge*).

ಅವನ ಕಣ್ಣಿಗೆ ಏನಾಗಿದೆ?	**avana kaṇṇige yên'âg' ide?**
What is the matter with his eye	his to eye what h. become is?
ಎರಡೂ ಕಣ್ಣು ಕಾಣುವದಿಲ್ಲ	**yeraḍû kaṇṇu kâṇuvad' illa**
He is blind on both eyes	two even eye the seeing is not
ಅಲ್ಲ, ಒಂದು ಕಣ್ಣು ಕಾಣುತ್ತದೆ	**alla, *w*ondu kaṇṇu kâṇuttade**
No, he can see with one eye	not so, one eye it sees
ನಿನ್ನ ಕಣ್ಣು ಕಾಣುವದಿಲ್ಲ? *S.* (...ಕಾಣುವದಿಲ್ಲವೋ? *C.*)	**ninna kaṇṇu kâṇuvad'illa?** *S.* (... **kâṇu-vad'illa-v-ô?** *C.*)
Have you no eyes? Are you blind?	thy eye the seeing is not? (..the seeing is not?)
ಕಷ್ಟದಿಂದ ಕಂಗೆಟ್ಟ	**kashṭadinda kaṅ' geṭṭa**[2]
He got confused by his troubles (...lost his sight...)	by trouble eye he became bad
ಅದನ್ನು ನೋಡಿ ಕಣ್ಣಿಗೆ ನೀರು ತಂದ	**adannu nôḍi kaṇṇige nîru tanda**
Seeing it he shed tears	that h. seen to the eye water he brought
ಬಹಳ ಕಣ್ಣೀರು ತಂದಳು	**bahaḷa kaṇ'ṇîru tandaḷu**
She shed many tears	much eye-water she brought
ನಿನ್ನ ಕಣ್ಣಿಗೇನು ಬಿತ್ತು?	**ninna kaṇṇig' ênu bittu?**
What did you perceive?	thy to the eye what it fell?
ನನ್ನ ಕಣ್ಣಿಗೆ ಒಂದು ಹೂವು ಬಿತ್ತು	**nanna kaṇṇige *w*ondu hûvu bittu**
I perceived a flower	my to the eye one flower it fell
ಅದರ ಮೇಲೆ ಕಣ್ಣಿಟ್ಟಿಯಾ? *S.* (...ಕಣ್ಣಿಟ್ಟಿಯೋ? *C.*)	**adara mêle kaṇṇ'iṭṭi-y-â?** *S.* (..**kaṇṇ iṭṭi-y-ô?** *C.*)
Have you an eye upon that?	on that eye thou setst? (...eye thou setst?

1 *Biḍu* is hear used instead of *baḍu=paḍu*, to suffer. Though this use of *biḍu* is very common, it is not to be imitated.

2 *Kaṅgeṭṭa=kaṇṇu* \| *keṭṭa*, for *keṭṭanu*, see section 41; literally, he became bad with respect to his eye; the latter *k* is for euphony's sake changed into *g*, and *ṇ* into *ṅ*.

47. ಬಾಯಿ bâyi=mouth (*G. Mund, Öffnung*).

ಅದನ್ನು ನೋಡಿದರೆ ಬಾಯಲ್ಲಿ ನೀರು ಬರುತ್ತವೆ	**adannu nôḍidare bâyalli nîru baruttave**[1]
One's mouth waters at the sight [of it	that if seen in the mouth water they [come
ಅದನ್ನು ಬಾಯೊಳಗೆ ಹಾಕಿಕೊಂಡ	**adannu bây' oḷage hâki koṇḍa**
He devoured it	that of the mouth within h. thrown he took
ಅಷ್ಟು ಬಾಯಿ ಮಾಡ ಬೇಡ	**ashṭu bâyi mâḍa bêḍa**
Do not bawl; do not talk so much	so much mouth to make is not wanted
ಬಾಯಿ ಮುಚ್ಚು	**bâyi mučču**
Hold your tongue	mouth shut
ಬಾಯಿ ಮಾಡಿ ಓದು	**bâyi mâḍi *w*ôdu**
Read aloud	mouth h. made read
ಈ ಮಗುವಿಗೆ ಬಾಯಿ ಬಂದದೋ? (...ಬಂದದೇನು? *S.*)	**î maguvige bâyi band'adô? (...ban-dad'ênu? *S.*)**
Can this child already speak?	this to the child mouth h. come is it? [(...it is what?)
ಇನ್ನೂ ಬಾಯಿ ಬಂದಿಲ್ಲ	**innû bâyi band' illa**
It cannot yet speak	yet mouth h. come is not
ಬಾಯಿಪಾಠ ಬರುತ್ತದೋ? (...ಬರುತ್ತದೇನು? *S.*)	**bâyipâṭha baruttadô? (...baruttad'-ênu? *S.*)**
Do you know it by heart? Can you recite your lesson?	mouth-lesson it comes? (...it comes [what?)
ನನ್ನ ಬಾಯಿಗೆ ಬರುವದಿಲ್ಲ	**nanna bâyige baruvad' illa**
I cannot recite it	my to mouth the coming is not
ಬಾಯಿಮಾತು	**bâyimâtu**
A verbal message; mere words	mouth-word

48. ಮಾಡು mâḍu=to do, to make (*G. tun, machen*).

ನೀ ಮಾಡಿದ ಕೆಲಸವೇನು? (ಕೆಲಸೇನು?)	**nî mâḍida kelasa-v-ênu? (...kelas' ênu?)**
What is the work you have done?	thou made work what?
ಆಕೆ ಏನೂ ಮಾಡಲಿಲ್ಲ, (...ಮಾಡಿಲ್ಲ)	**âke *y*ênû mâḍal'illa, (...mâḍ'illa)**
She has not done anything	she what even to do is not (...h. done is not)
ಏನು ಮಾಡ್ಯಾಳು?	***y*ênu mâḍyâḷu?**
What could she do?	what she will do?

[1] *Nîru*, though singular, is commonly followed by a verb in the plural.

ಕೆಲಸ ಮಾಡದೆ ಮನೆಗೆ ಹೋದಳು	**kelasa mâḍade manege hôdaḷu**
She went home without doing her work	work not h. done to the house she went
ಆಕೆ ಏನೂ ಮಾಡುವ ಹಾಗಿಲ್ಲ	**âke yênû mâḍuva hâg'illa**
She is not likely to do anything	she what even doing like is not
ಈಕೆ ಕೆಲಸ ಮಾಡುವಾಕೆ ಅಲ್ಲ	**îke kelasa mâḍuv'âke alla**
She is not fond of work; she is not a working person	she work doing she not
ಕೆಲಸ ಮಾಡದವರು ಉಣ್ಣ ಬಾರದು	**kelasa mâḍad' avaru uṇṇa bâradu**[1]
Those that will not work (...have not worked) shall not eat	work not doing they to eat it will not come
ಚಲೋ ಮಾಡುತ್ತೀರಿ	**čalô mâḍuttîri**
You do quite right	nice you do
ಬಹಳ ರಾತ್ರಿ ಮಾಡಿ ಬಂದ	**bahaḷa râtri mâḍi banda**
He came late in the night	much night h. made he came
ಕುದುರೆ ಮಾಡಿಕೊಂಡು ಬಂದ	**kudure mâḍi koṇḍu banda**
He hired a horse and came on horseback	a horse h. made h. taken he came

49. ಸಾಲು **sâlu** = to be enough, to suffice (*G. hinreichen, genug sein*).

An Old Kanarese form of this verb is s â k u[2] (instead of s â l k u; compare b ê k u No. 15), used for all persons, genders and numbers in the present tense; as, n â n u s â k u = I am enough, n î v u s â k u = you are enough, a d u s â k u = it is enough. Combined with â g u it forms a new verb; s â k â g u t t ê n e, etc. = I suffice, am enough. As to the negative mood of s â k u see No. 13.

ಈ ನೀರು ಸಾಲದು (...ಸಾಲುವದಿಲ್ಲ)	**î nîru sâladu (...sâluvad'illa)**
This water is not sufficient	this water it will not suffice (...the sufficing is not)
ಸಾಲದಿದ್ದರೆ ಇನ್ನೂ ತರುತ್ತೇನೆ	**sâlad' iddare inn'û taruttêne**
If not sufficient, I shall bring more	not being enough if been more also I bring
ಸಾಕಾಗುವಷ್ಟು ತಾ	**sâk'aguv' ashṭu tâ**
Bring enough of it	sufficing that much bring
ಎಷ್ಟು ತಂದರೂ ನಿಮಗೆ ಸಾಲುವದಿಲ್ಲ	**yeshṭu tandur'û nimage sâluvad'illa**
Though I bring you ever so much, it is not enough	how much if brought even to you the sufficing is not

---

[1] See note 5, p. 34.

[2] See note 4, p. 34. The word *sâku* is used in all genders and numbers of the 3rd present and future.

ಇಷ್ಟಾದರೆ ಸಾಕು — isht'âdare sâku
This much will do — this much if become is enough

ಹತ್ತು ಮಂದಿ ಸಾಕಾದರೇನು? *S.* (...ಸಾಕಾದರೋ? *C.*) — hattu mandi sâkâdar'ênu? *S.* (... sâk' âdar'ô? *C.*)
Where ten people enough — ten people sufficed what? (...sufficed)?

ಸಾಲಲಿಲ್ಲ, *or* ಸಾಕಾಗಲಿಲ್ಲ — sâlal' illa, *or* sâkâgal' illa
They were not enough — to suffice is not

ಇಪ್ಪತ್ತು ಮಂದಿ ಸಾಲಲಿಕ್ಕಿಲ್ಲ (...ಸಾಕಾಗಲಿಕ್ಕಿಲ್ಲ) — ippattu mandi sâlalikk' illa (... sâk'âgalikk' illa
Twenty people will not be sufficient — twenty people to suffice is not

ಈಗ ಸಾಕು [enough — îga sâku
Now it is enough, now there are — now it is enough

ಸಾಕಂತೆ — sâk' ante
It is enough he says — enough it says

50. ಕೊಡು koḍu = to give (*G. geben.* See No. 41).

ಅವನಿಗೊಂದು ಗಾಡಿ ಮಾಡಿ ಕೊಟ್ಟೆ — avanig'ondu gâḍi mâḍi koṭṭe
I made a carriage for him — to him one carriage h. made I gave

ರೂಪಾಯಿ ಕೊಟ್ಟನೇನು? *S.* (...ಕೊಟ್ಟನೋ? *C*) — rûpâyi koṭṭan'ênu? *S.* (...kôṭṭanô? *C.*)
Has he paid it? — rupee he gave what? (...he gave?)

ಎಲ್ಲಿಂದ ಕೊಟ್ಟಾನು? [How...? — yellinda koṭṭânu?
Wherefrom should he pay it? — whence he will give?

ಅವನು ಕೊಡಲಿಕ್ಕಿಲ್ಲ — avanu koḍalikk'illa
He won't pay — he to give is not

ಕೊಡದಿದ್ದರೆ, ನಾನೇ ಕೊಡಿಸುತ್ತೇನೆ — koḍad' iddare, nânê koḍisuttêne
If he should not pay, I myself shall make him pay — not h. given if been, / I shall cause to give

ಅವರಪ್ಪ ಕೊಡಿಸಿದನು — avar' appa koḍisidanu
His father made him pay — their father he caused to give

ನೂರು ರೂಪಾಯಿ ಕಳುಹಿಸಿ ಕೊಟ್ಟ — nûru rûpâyi kaḷuhisi koṭṭa
He sent a hundred rupees — hundred rupee h. sent he gave

ಈ ಎತ್ತು ನನಗೆ ಬಹಳ ಕಷ್ಟ ಕೊಡುತ್ತದೆ — î yettu nanage bahaḷa kashṭa koḍuttade
This bullock gives me a good deal of trouble — this bullock to me much trouble it gives

ನನಗೂ ಬಹಳ ಕೊಟ್ಟಿತು	**nanag'û bahaḷa koṭṭitu**
It gave me also a good deal	to me also much it gave
ಹತ್ತರ ಬರಗೊಡಿಸುವದಿಲ್ಲ ... (ಗೊಡುವದಿಲ್ಲ)	**hattara bara goḍisuvad'illa**[1] (... **goḍuvad'illa**)
It lets no one come near it	near to come the causing to give is not (...the giving is not)

51. ರೆ re=if (*G. wenn*); ಊ û=too, also, even (*G. auch*); ರೂ rû (re+û)=though (*G. obgleich*).

Re is an abbreviation of the Old Kanarese word aḍe or oḍe sometimes written are, which may again be derived from oḍa=union, junction; oḍe=in the union, at the junction, at the same time; hôguvaḍe or hôdaḍe=at the time of going. Being a noun, the word was originally joined to any participle now it is only added as an affix to the past relative participle of *if*. Combined with the participle âda (from âgu) as âdare, it often gives it the meaning of *but*.

ಅವನನ್ನು (ಅವನ್ನ) ಕಳುಹಿಸಿದರೆ, ಹೋಗುತ್ತಾನೆ	avanannu (avanna) **kaḷuhisidare, hôguttâne**
If you (*a. p.*) send him, he will go	him if sent, he goes
ಒಂದು ರೂಪಾಯಿ ಕೊಟ್ಟರೆ, ಹೋಗುತ್ತಾರಂತೆ	**wondu rûpâyi koṭṭare, hôguttâr' ante**
They will go for a rupee I hear	one rupee is given, they go it says
ಎರಡು ಕೊಟ್ಟರೂ ಹೋಗಲಿಕ್ಕಿಲ್ಲ	**yeraḍu koṭṭarû hôgalikk' illa**
They would not go for two	two if given even to go is not
ಮೂರಾದರೆ ಹೋದಾರು	**mûr' âdare hôdâru**
They might go for three	three if become they will go
ಆದರೆ ಅವರು ಈ ಹೊತ್ತು ಹೋಗುವ ಹಾಗಿಲ್ಲ	**âdare avaru î hottu hôguva hâg' illa**
But to-day they cannot go	but they this time going like is not
ಹೋಗುತ್ತೇವೆಂದರೂ ಹೋಗುವದಿಲ್ಲ	**hôguttêv'andarû hôguvad' illa**
They will not go though they promise it	we go if said even the going is not
ಅವನಾದರೆ ಹೋಗುತ್ತಾನೆ	**avan'âdare hôguttâne**
As to him, he will go	he if become he goes

[1] *Goḍisuvadu* and *goḍuvadu* for *koḍisuvadu* and *koḍuvadu; k* changed into *g* for euphony's sake. Both these forms are used indiscriminately in the sense of the English auxiliary "to let".

ಹೋಗುವವರು ಯಾರ್ಯಾರಂದರೆ	**hôguv'avaru yâr' yâr' andare**
The following persons are going (...will go)	going they who who if said
ನಾನೂ ಇವನೂ ಅವನೂ	**nânû, ivanû, avanû**
Myself, this one and that one	I too he too he too
ಬೇಕಾದರೆ ನಮ್ಮಪ್ಪನೂ ಹೋದಾನು	**bêk'âdare namm'appan'û hôdânu**
If necessary my father will go too	if it is wanted our father too he will go

52. ಇಂತ, ಇಂತಲು **inta, intalu** = than (*G. als*), follows the Dative Case.

The Comparative and Superlative Degrees

ಅವ(ನು) ನನಗಿಂತ ದೊಡ್ಡವ(ನು)	**ava(nu) nanag'inta doḍḍava(nu)**
He is taller (older, richer) than I	he than I greater
ಇವ ಎಲ್ಲರಿಗಿಂತಲೂ ಚಿಕ್ಕವ	**iva yellarig'intal'û čikk'ava**
He is smaller (younger) than all; ...the youngest of all	he than all even little
ಇವನು ಎಲ್ಲರಲ್ಲಿ ಚಿಕ್ಕವ	**ivanu yellaralli čikkava**
He is the youngest of all	he in all little
ಆದರೂ ಎಲ್ಲರಿಗಿಂತ ಕೆಟ್ಟವ	**âdarû yellarig'inta keṭṭava**
But he is the worst of all	though than all bad
ಅವನಿಗಿಂತ ಕೆಟ್ಟವರಿಲ್ಲ	**avanig'inta keṭṭa'var' illa**
There are none worse than he	than he bad ones are not
ನಮಗಿಂತ ಮುಂಚೆ ಬಂದಿದ್ದ	**namag'inta munče band' idda**
He had arrived before us	than we before h. come he was
ನಮ್ಮ ಕುದುರೆಗಿಂತ ನಿಮ್ಮದು ಚಲೋದು	**namma kudureg'inta nimmadu čalôdu**
Your horse is better than ours	our than horse yours nice
ನೀವು ನಮಗಿಂತ ಹೆಚ್ಚು ಕೊಟ್ಟಿರಿ	**nîvu namag' inta hečču koṭṭiri**
You paid more than we	you than we more you gave
ನೂರಕ್ಕಿಂತ ಹೆಚ್ಚು ಕೊಟ್ಟೆವು	**nûrakk'inta hečču koṭṭevu**
We paid more than a hundred	than hundred more we gave
ಇದಕ್ಕಿಂತಲೂ ಹೆಚ್ಚು ಕೊಡ ಬಹುದಿತ್ತು	**idakk'intal'û hečču koḍa bahud' ittu**[1]
You might have given even more than that	than this even more to give it was possible

[1] See Note 5, p. 34.

53. ಹೌದು **houdu**=yes, for **ahudu**=**âguvadu** (*G. ja*)

ಅದನ್ನು ಯಾರು ಹೇಳಿದರು?	**adannu yâru hêḷidaru?**
Who said that? who told you that?	that who they said? [ô? C.)
ನೀನು ಹೇಳಿದಿ, ಹೌದಲ್ಲ? *S*.(...ಅಲ್ಲವೋ? *C*)	**nînu hêḷidi, houd'alla?** *S*. (...allav'
You said it, did you not?	thou saidst, yes not? (...not?)
ಹೌದಾದರೆ ಹೇಳು	**houd'âdare hêḷu**
If it be so, tell it	yes if become say
ಹೌದಾದರೆ ಹೌದನ್ನು	**houd'âdare houd'annu**
If it be so, say yes	yes if become yes say
ನೀ ಹೇಳಿದ್ದು ಹೌದೇನು? (...ಹೌದೋ?)	**nî hêḷiddu houd'ênu?** (...**houd'ô?**)
Is it true that you told it?	thou the h. said yes what? (...yes?)
ಹೌದಪ್ಪಾ, ನಾ ಹೇಳಿದೆ	**houd'appâ, nâ hêḷide**
Yes sir, I told it	yes father ,I I said
ನೀನೇ ಹೌದೋ?	**nînê houd'ô?**
Is it really you? was it...?	*thou* yes?
ನಾನೇ ಹೌದು, *or* ಹೌದು ನಾನೇ	**nânê houdu**, *or* **houdu nânê**
Yes, it is I	*I* yes, yes *I*
ಹೌದಂದ	**houd'anda**
He said yes; he has confessed it	yes he said
ಹೌದೋ ಅಲ್ಲೋ ಯಾರಿಗೆ ಗೊತ್ತು?	**houd'ô all'ô yârige gottu?**
Who knows if it be true or not?	yes? not? to whom certainty?

54. ಹೇಳು **hêḷu**=to say, to tell (*G. sagen*). See also ಅನ್ನು **annu**, No. 3.

ಅವನಿಗೆ ಯಾವ ಮಾತ್ಹೇಳಿದಿರಿ?	**avanige yâva mât' hêḷidiri?**
What did you tell him?	to him which word you told?
ಅವನಿಗೇನೆಂತ ಹೇಳಲಿ?	**avanig' ên' enta hêḷali?**
What am I to tell him?	to him what saying let (*a. p.*) say?
ನಮ್ಮಲ್ಲಿಗೆ ಬರಬೇಕೆಂತ (ಬೇಕೆಂದು) ಹೇಳಿರಿ	**namm'allige bara bêk'enta (..bêk' endu)**[1] **heḷiri**
Tell him to come to me	our thither to come it is wanted saying (...h. said) say
ಹೇಳುತ್ತೇನೆ	**hêḷuttêne**
I shall tell him (*a. p.*)	I tell

[1] See note 4, p. 54.

ಹೇಳಿ ಕಳುಹಿಸುತ್ತೇನೆ	hêḷi kaḷuhisuttêne
I shall send him word	h. said I send
ಅವರು ಅನ್ನುವದೇನು?	avaru annuvad' ênu?
What do they (does he) say?	they the saying what?
ಏನೆಂತ ಹೇಳಿ ಕಳುಹಿಸಿದರು?	yen'ênta hêḷi kaḷuhisidaru?
What answer did they send?	what saying h. said they sent?
ಬರುವದಿಲ್ಲನ್ನುತ್ತಾರೆ	baruvad' ill' annuttâre
They say they will not come; he says he...	the coming is not they say
ಅವರು ಏನೂ ಹೇಳಲಿಲ್ಲ	avaru yên'û hêḷal' illa
They (he) did not say anything	they what even to say is not
ಹೇಳಿಕೊಳ್ಳುವ ಮಾತದೆ	hêḷi koḷḷuva mât' ade
I have something to say	h. said taking word it is

55. ಕೇಳು kêḷu=to hear, to ask (*G. hören, fragen*).

ಘಂಟೆ ಬಾರಿಸಿದ್ದನ್ನು ಕೇಳಿದಿಯೇನು? *S.* (...ಕೇಳಿದಿಯೋ? *C.*)	ghaṇṭe bârisiddannu kêḷidi-y-ênu? *S.* (...kêḷidi-yô? *C.*)
Did you hear the bell ring?	bell the h. rung thou heardst what? (...thou heardst?)
(ನಾ) ಕೇಳಲಿಲ್ಲ	(nâ) kêḷal' illa
I did not hear it	(I) to hear is not
ನಿನ್ನ ಕಿವಿ ಕೇಳುವದಿಲ್ಲೇನು? *S.* (ಕೇಳುವದಿಲ್ಲವೋ? *C.*)	ninna kivi keḷuvad'ill'ènu? *S.* (...kêḷuvad'illa-v-ô? *C.*)
Are you deaf?	thy ear the hearing is not what? (...the hearing is not)
ಕಿವಿ ಕೇಳುತ್ತದೆ	kivi kêḷuttade
I am not deaf; I can hear	ear it hears
ಅವರು ಘಂಟೆ ಕೇಳಿದರೇನು? *S.* (...ಕೇಳಿದರೋ? *C.*)	avaru ghaṇṭe kêḷidar' ênu? *S.* (...kêḷi- dar'ô? *C.*)
Did they (he) hear the bell?	they bell they heard what? (...they heard?)
ಹೋಗಿ ಕೇಳಿರಿ	hôgi kêḷiri
Go and ask	h. gone ask
ಕೇಳಿಕೊಂಡು ಬರ್ರಿ *S.* (...ಬನ್ನಿ *C.*)	kêḷi koṇḍu barri *S.* (...banni *C.*)
Go and ask	h. asked h. taken come (...come)
ನೀವು ಹೇಳಿದ ಹಾಗೆ ಕೇಳುತ್ತೇನೆ	nîvu hêḷida hâge kêḷuttêne
I shall obey your orders	you which said like I hear

ಎಲ್ಲಿ ಕೇಳುತ್ತೀರಿ? [obey	**yelli keḷuttîri?**
You obey, do you? *i. e.* You never	where you hear?
ನೀವು ಮಾತು ಕೇಳುವವರಲ್ಲ	**nîvu mâtu kêḷuv'avar' alla**
You are not obedient	you word hearing ones not

56. ನಿಲ್ಲು **nillu**=to stand, to wait (*G. stehen, waten*). See No. 41.

ಎದ್ದು ನಿಂದಿರ್ರಿ *or* ಎದ್ದ್ ನಿಂದಿರ್ರಿ	**yeddu nind'irri** *ov* **yedd nind'irri**
Stand up	h. risen h. stood be
ನಾವು ಬರುವ ತನಕ ನಿಲ್ಲಬೇಕು	**nâvu baruva tanaka nilla bêku**
Wait till we (I) come	we coming till to stand it is wanted
ಸ್ವಲ್ಪ ನಿಂತು ಬರುತ್ತೇವೆ	**svalpa nintu baruttêve**
We are coming soon	little h. stood we come
ಇಲ್ಲಿ ಯಾಕೆ ನಿಂತಿರುತ್ತೀರಿ?	**illi yâke nint' iruttîri?**
Why are you standing here?	here why h. stood you are?
ನಮ್ಮನ್ನಿಲ್ಲಿ ನಿಂದಿರಿಸಿದರು	**nammann'illi nind'irisidaru**[1]
They made us stand here; we have been placed here	us here h. stood they caused to be
ಕೆಲಸ ನಿಂತ್ಹೋಯಿತು	**kelasa nint' hôyitu**
Work has ceased;..has been stopped	work h. stood it went
ಅದನ್ನು ನಿಲ್ಲಿಸಿಬಿಟ್ಟರು	**adannu nillisi biṭṭaru**
It has been entirely stopped	that h. caused to stand they left
ಯಾಕೆ ನಿಲ್ಲಿಸಿದ್ದಾರೆ?	**yâke nillis' iddhâre?**
Why has it been stopped?	why h. caused to stand they are?
ನೀರು ಬಹಳ ನಿಂದಿರುತ್ತದೆ, ಅದಕ್ಕೆ	**nîru bahaḷa nind' iruttade, adakke**
Because there is plenty of water standing there	water much h. stood it is, to that
ನಿಲ್ಲಲಿಕ್ಕಾಗುವದಿಲ್ಲ, ಹೋಗುತ್ತೇನೆ	**nillalikk'âguvad' illa, hôguttêne**
I cannot wait, I am going	to stand the becoming is not, I go

57. ಮೇಲೆ **mêle**=on, after, above, up (*G. auf, oben, hinauf*).

The following cases of this adverb, which in fact is a kind of locative case of the noun **m ê l u**=the upper part, are still in use—

[1] *Irisidaru*, causative form of *iru*.

Instr. **mêlinda, mêlininda,** from above *Gen.* **mêlina,** upper
Dat. **mêlakke,** upwards *Loc.* **mêle,** above

ಯಾವ ಮನೆ ನಿಮ್ಮದು, ಮೇಲಿನದೋ? ಕೆಳಗಿನದೋ?	**yâva mane nimmadu, mêlin'adô? keḷagin'adô?**[1]
Which is your house, the upper one or the lower one?	which house yours, upper one? lower one?
ಮೇಲಿನ ಮನೆ ನಮ್ಮದು	**mêlina mane nammadu**
The upper one is ours	upper house ours
ಮೇಲೆ ಹೋಗುತ್ತೀರೇನು? *S.* (...ಹೋಗುತ್ತೀರೋ? *C.*)	**mêle hôguttîr'ênu?** *S.* (...**hôguttîr'ô?** *C.*)
Are you going up? *or*, will you go up	up you go what? (you go?)
ಇದೇ ಈಗ ಮೇಲಿಂದ (ಮೇಲಿನಿಂದ) ಬಂದೆ	**idê îga**[2] **mêlinda (mêlininda) bande**
I am just coming from above	just now from above I came
ನಮ್ಮಣ್ಣ ಮೇಲೆ ಇರುತ್ತಾನೆ	**namm'aṇṇa mêle iruttâne**
My brother is above; ...up there	our elder brother above he is
ಆತನು ಬಂದ ಮೇಲೆ ಹೋಗುತ್ತೇನೆ	**âtanu banda mêle hôguttêne**
After his arrival I shall go	after he came I go
ಆ ಮೇಲೆ ಹೋಗಲಿಕ್ಕಾಗುತ್ತದೆ	**â mêle hôgalikk'âguttade**
After that it is possible to go; *or*, afterwards	that after to go it becomes
ನಾಲ್ಕು ದಿವಸದ ಮೇಲೆ ಬಂದಾನು	**nâlku divasada mêle bandânu**
He will probably come after some [days	four of day after he may come
ಕುದುರೆಯ ಮೇಲೆ ಬಂದಾರು	**kudureya mêle bandâru**
They (he) will probably come on horseback	of the horse on they may come
ಇನ್ನು ಮೇಲೆ ಬರಲಿಕ್ಕಿಲ್ಲ	**innu mêle baralikk'illa**
He will not come hereafter; *or*, in future he will not	more after to come is not

58. ಕೂಡ್ರು, ಕುಂಡ್ರು, ಕೂತುಕೊಳ್ಳು **kûḍru**[3], **kuṇḍru, kûtukoḷḷu** = to sit down (*G. sich setzen, sitzen*) As to its conjugation see No. 41.

ಇಲ್ಲಿ ಬಂದು ಕೂತುಕೊಳ್ಳಿರಿ	**illi bandu kûtu koḷḷiri**
Come here and sit down	here h. come h. sat down take

1 See Rem. 2, No. 6.

2 *Idê* = *idu* + *ê* = just this; combined with *îga* it signifies "just now".

3 The forms with *ṇ* or *n* are considered vulgar.

ಅಲ್ಲಿ ಯಾಕೆ ಕೂತಿರುತ್ತೀರಿ? (...ಕುಂತಿರುತ್ತೀರಿ?)	alli yâke kût' iruttîri? (kunt' iruttî- ri[1]?)
Why are you sitting there?	there why h. sat you are?
ಎಲ್ಲಿ ಕೂಡ್ರಲಿ? (...ಕುಂಡ್ರಲಿ?) [sit?	yelli kûḍrali? (...kuṇḍrali[1]?)
Where shall I sit? where am I to	where let (*a. p.*) sit down?
ಕೆಳಗೆ ಕೂಡ್ರ (ಕುಂಡ್ರ) ಬೇಡ, ಮೇಲೆ ಕೂಡ್ರಿ (ಕುಂಡ್ರಿ) [sit up here	keḷage kûḍra (kuṇḍra[1]) béḍa, mêle kûḍri[2] (kuṇḍri[1])
Do not sit on the ground (below),	down to sit is not wanted, up sit down
ಎಲ್ಲಿ ಕೂತರೂ (ಕುಂತರೂ) ಒಂದೇ [sit	yelli kûtar'û (kuntar'û[1]) wondê
It does not matter where we (*a. p.*)	where if sat even *one*
ನೀವು ಹೇಳಿದಲ್ಲಿ ಕೂಡ್ರುತ್ತೇನೆ (...ಕುಂಡ್ರುತ್ತೇನೆ) [to sit	nîvu hêḷid'alli kûḍruttêne (...kuṇḍruttêne[1])
I shall sit down where you tell me	which you told there I sit down
ರಾತ್ರಿಯೆಲ್ಲಾ ಕೂತು ಏನು ಮಾಡಿದಿ?	râtri-y-ellâ kûtu yênu mâḍidi?
What were you doing sitting up all night?	night all h. sat what thou didst?
ನಾ ಕೂತುಕೊಂಡಿದ್ದಿಲ್ಲ	nâ kûtukoṇḍ' idd' illa
I was not sitting up	I h. sat down h. been is not
ನಾ ರಾತ್ರಿಯಲ್ಲಿ ಕೂತುಕೊಳ್ಳುವವನಲ್ಲ	nâ râtriyalli kûtukoḷḷuv'avan'alla
I am not one who sits up at night	I in the night a sitting up person not
ಇದು ಕೂಡ್ರುವ ಮನೆ	idu kûḍruva mane
This is the sitting room	this sitting house

59. ಏಳು **yêḷu** = to rise, to get up (G. *aufstehen*). See No. 41.

ಏಳೇಳು	yêḷ' êḷu
Rise! get up!	rise rise
ಎಲ್ಲರೂ ಏಳಲಿ	yellar'û yêḷali
Let every one rise	all even let (*a. p.*) rise
ಎದ್ದೇನು ಮಾಡಲಿ?	yedd' ênu mâḍali?
What are we to do after getting up?	h. risen what let (*a. p.*) do?
ಎದ್ದ ಮೇಲೆ ನೀರು ತರಬೇಕು	yeḍda mêle nîru tara bêku
After getting up you will have to fetch water	risen after water to fetch is wanted

[1] The forms with *ṇ* or *n* are considered vulgar.

[2] Instead of *kûdriri*.

ಇನ್ನೂ ಯಾರೂ ಎದ್ದಿಲ್ಲ	innû yâr'û yedd' illa
No one has risen yet	yet even who even h. risen are not
ಯಾರೂ ಏಳುವದಿಲ್ಲ	yâr'û yêḷuvad' illa
Ne one is getting up	who even the rising is not
ಆರು ಘಂಟೆಗೇಳುತ್ತಾರೆ	âru ghaṇṭeg' êḷuttâre
They get up at six o'clock	six to the bell they rise [iruttâre)
ಅಷ್ಟರೂ ಎದ್ದಿದ್ದಾರೆ (...ಎದ್ದಿರುತ್ತಾರೆ)	ashṭar'û yedd' iddâre (...yedd'-
They have all risen	all h. risen they are
ಎದ್ದು ಬಹಳ ಹೊತ್ತಾಯಿತು	yeddu bahaḷa hott' âyitu
They got up long ago	h. risen much time it became
ನಾ ಮಾತ್ರ ಏಳಲಾರೆ	nâ mâtra yêḷal' âre
As for me I cannot rise	I only to rise I cannot

60. ಬೀಳು bîḷu = to fall (*G. fallen*). See No. 41.

ಈ ರೂಪಾಯಿ ಎಲ್ಲಿ ಕಂಡುಕೊಂಡಿ?	î rûpâyi yêlli kaṇḍu koṇḍi?
Whare did you find this rupee?	this rupee where h. seen thou tookst?
ನನ್ನ ಮನೆಯಲ್ಲಿ ಬಿದ್ದಿತ್ತು	nanna maneyalli bidd' ittu
It was lying in my house	my in the house h. fallen it was
ಮನೆಗೆ ಬಂದಾಗಲೇ ಕಣ್ಣಿಗೆ ಬಿತ್ತು	manege band'âgal'ê kaṇṇige bittu
It caught my eye as soon as I came home	to the house *that time* which (I) came to the eye it fell
ತಂಗಿ ಬೀಳುತ್ತಾಳೆ, ನೋಡು	taṅgi bîḷuttâḷe, nôḍu
Look, your sister will fall; ...the little girl...	younger sister she falls, look
ಆಕೆಯನ್ನು ಬೀಳಗೊಡುವದಿಲ್ಲ	âkeyannu bîḷagoḍuvad' illa
I shall not let her fall	her to fall the giving is not
ಬೀಳದ ಹಾಗೆ ನೋಡುತ್ತೇನೆ [falling	bîḷada hâge nôḍuttêne
I shall take care to keep her from	not falling like I see [bidda
ನಿಮ್ಮಣ್ಣ ಕೆಟ್ಟವರ ಕೈಯಲ್ಲಿ ಬಿದ್ದ	nimm' aṇṇa keṭṭ'avara keiyalli
Your brother has fallen into the hands of bad men	your elder brother of bad ones in the hand he fell
ರಾತ್ರಿಯಲ್ಲಿ ಅವನ ಮೇಲೆ ಬಿದ್ದರು	râtriyalli avana mêle biddaru
They fell on him at night; they attacked him... [ಬಿದ್ದಿತ್ತೋ?)	in the night his on they fell [ênu? (bidd'itt'ô?)
ಈ ಮಾತು ನಿಮ್ಮ ಕಿವಿಗೆ ಬಿದ್ದಿತ್ತೇನು? (...	î mâtu nimma kivige bidd'itt'
Had you heard of this matter?	this word your to the ear h. fallen it was what? (h. fallen it was?)

ನನ್ನ ಕಿವಿಗೆ ಬಿದ್ದಿದ್ದಿಲ್ಲ	**nanna kivige bidd' idd' illa**
I had not heard of it	my to the ear h. fallen h. been is not

61. ತರು **taru** = to bring (*G. bringen*) See No. 41.

ನೀರು ತಾ	**nîru[1] tâ**
Fetch me some water	water bring
ಎಷ್ಟು ತರಲಿ?	**yeshṭu tarali?**
How much shall I bring?	how much let (*a. p.*) bring?
ಒಂದು ಸ್ವಲ್ಪ ತಂದು ಹಾಕು	**wondu svalpa tandu hâku**
Bring a little and pour it (in here)	one little h. brought throw
ನಮ್ಮ ತಮ್ಮ ತರುತ್ತಾನೆ	**namma tamma taruttâne**
My brother will bring some	our younger brother brings
ಅವ ಯಾವಾಗ ತಂದಾನು?	**ava yâvâga tandânu?**
When will he bring it?	he when he will bring?
ಅವ ತರಲಿಕ್ಕಿಲ್ಲ, *or* ಅವ ತರುವದಿಲ್ಲ	**ava taralikk'illa,** *or* **ava taruvad'illa**
He will not bring any (it)	he to bring is not, he the bringing is not
ಅವ ತಾರದಿದ್ದರೆ, ನಾ ತರುತ್ತೇನೆ	**ava târad' iddare[2], nâ taruttêne**
If he will not bring any, I will	he not bringing if been, I bring
ಆ ಕತ್ತೀ ತಂದು ತೋರಿಸಿರಿ	**â kattî tandu tôrisiri**
Show me that knife (sword)	that knife h. brought show
ತಂದಿದ್ದೇನೆ ನೋಡಿರಿ	**tand' iddhêne, nôḍiri**
Look here, I have brought it	h. brought I am, look
ಅದನ್ನು ಇಲ್ಲಿ ತರ್ರಿ *S.* (...ತನ್ನಿ *C.*)	**adannu illi tarri** *S.* (...**tanni** *C.*)
Hand it to me	it here bring (*pl.*), (bring *pl.*)

62. ಇಲ್ಲಿ **illi** = here (*G. hier*); ಅಲ್ಲಿ **alli** = there (*G. dort*); ಎಲ್ಲಿ **yelli** = where? (*G. wo?*).

These adverbs are to be considered as locative cases of nouns; the cases still in use are—·

---

[1] See note 2, p. 57. Colloquially the phrase *nîra tâ* (perhaps an abbreviation of *takkoṇḍu tâ*) is common.

[2] Some spell *tarad'iddare.*

Instr.	**illinda,**	**allinda,**	**yellinda.**
Dat.	**illige,**	**allige,**	**yellige.**
Gen.	**illiya**	**alliya,**	**yelliya,** *or* **illi** etc.
Loc.	**illi,**	**alli,**	**yelli.**

ನಿಮ್ಮಣ್ಣ ಎಲ್ಲಿರುತ್ತಾನೆ?	**nimm'aṇṇa yell' iruttâne?**
Where is your brother?	your elder brother where he is?
ಇಲ್ಲಿ ಇಲ್ಲ, ಅಲ್ಲಿರುತ್ತಾನೆ	**illi illa, all' iruttâne**
He is not here, he is there	here he is not, there he is
ಎಲ್ಲಿ (*or* ಎಲ್ಲಿಗೆ) ಹೋದನು?	**yelli** (*or* **yellige**) **hôdanu?**
Where has he gone?	where (whither) he went?
ಎಲ್ಲಿಯೋ ಹೋಗಿದ್ಧಾನೆ	**yelliyô hôg' iddhâne**
I do not know where he has gone	whither? h. gone he is
ಇಲ್ಲಿ ಇಲ್ಲ, ಎಲ್ಲಿಯೂ ಇಲ್ಲ	**illi illa, yelli-y-û illa**
He is neither here nor anywhere else	here not, where even he is not
ಎಲ್ಲೆಲ್ಲಿ ನೋಡಿದರೂ ಕಾಣುವದಿಲ್ಲ	**yell'elli nôḍidar'û kâṇuvad'illa**
I cannot find him anywhere	where where if seen even the appearing is not
ಎಲ್ಲಿಂದ ಬಂದಿರಿ?	**yellinda bandiri?**
Where are you come from?	whence you came?
ನೀವು ಎಲ್ಲಿಯವರು?	**nîvu yelliy' avaru?**
Where are you from?	you of where they?
ಅಲ್ಲಿಂದ ಬಂದೆವು	**allinda bandevu**
We have come from that place	thence we came
ನಾವು ಇಲ್ಲಿಯವರು	**nâvu illiy' avaru**
We belong to this place	we of here they

63. *The same continued.*

ಇಲ್ಲಿಯವರು ಅಲ್ಲಿ(ಗೆ) ಹೋಗುವ ಹಾಗಿಲ್ಲ	**illiy' avaru alli(ge) hôguva hâg'illa**
The people of this place cannot go there	of here they thither going like not
ಅಲ್ಲಿಯವರು ಇಲ್ಲಿ(ಗೆ) ಬರುವ ಹಾಗಿಲ್ಲ	**alliy' avaru illi(ge) baṛuva hâg' illa**
The people of that place cannot come here	of there they hither coming like not
ಅಲ್ಲಿಂದ ಇಲ್ಲಿಗೆ ಎಷ್ಟು ದೂರ?	**allinda illige yeshṭu dûra?**
How far is it from that place to this?	thence hither how much far?

ನೀನು ಇರುವದು ಎಲ್ಲಿ?	**nînu iruvadu yelli?**
Where do you live?	they being where?
ನೀನಿದ್ದಲ್ಲಿ ನಾ ಇರುತ್ತೇನೆ	**nîn' idd' alli nâ iruttêne**
I shall live where you live	that place where thou art I am
ನಾ ಹೋಗುವಲ್ಲಿಗೆ ನೀವು ಬರಲಾರಿರಿ	**nâ hôguv'allige nîvu baral' âriri**
You cannot come where I go	thither where I go you to come you cannot
ಕುದುರೆ ಎಲ್ಲಿತ್ತು?	**kudure yell' ittu?**
Where had the horse been?	horse where it was?
ನೀವು ಹೇಳಿದಲ್ಲಿಯೇ ಇತ್ತು	**nîvu hêḷid' alli-y-ê ittu**
It had been at the place which you mentioned	*at the place* you said it was
ಇಂಥಾ ಕುದುರೆಗಳು ಎಲ್ಲಿರುತ್ತವೆ?	**inthâ kuduregaḷu yell' iruttave?**
Where are horses like this to be had?	such horses where they are?
ಅಲ್ಲಲ್ಲಿರುತ್ತವೆ	**all' all' iruttave**
They are found here and there	there there they are

64. ಅಪ್ಪ, ತಂದೆ **appa, tande** = father (*G. Vater*);
ಅವ್ವ, ತಾಯಿ **avva, tâyi** = mother (*G. mutter*).

Appa and avva are declined like ava No. 4; but the plural is appandiru, avvandiru, and the honorary plural appanavaru, avvanavaru; tande and tâyi are declined like kei, see No. 19; plural tandegaḷu, tandeyavaru; tâyigaḷu, tâyandiru, tâyavaru. Aṇṇa, tamma and akka follow appa in their declension; taṅgi follows tâyi.

ಯಾಕಪ್ಪಾ, ಈ ಮನೆಯಲ್ಲಿ ಯಾರೂ ಇಲ್ಲ?	**yâk' appâ, î maneyalli yâr'û illa?**
Ho, is there no one at home?	why father, this in the house who even is not?
ಏನು ಬಾಲಪ್ಪನವರೇ, ನೀವು ಬಂದಿರೋ?	**yênu bâl'appanavarê, nîvu bandirô?**
What, Mr. Bâlappa! are you come?	what Bâlappa, you came?
ನಿಮ್ಮ ತಂದೆತಾಯಿಗಳು ಎಲ್ಲಿ?	**nimma tandetâyigaḷu[1] yelli?**
Where are your parents?	your parents where?
ನಮ್ಮಪ್ಪ *S.* (ನಮ್ಮ ತಂದೆ *C.*) ಊರಿಗೆ ಹೋಗಿದ್ದಾನೆ	**namm'appa** *S.* (**namma tande** *C.*) **ûrige hôg'iddâne**
My father has gone abroad	our father to town h. gone he is

[1] *Tandetâyigaḷu* = parents, is treated as one word and declined as such; as, *tandetâyigaḷannu*, *tandetâyigaḷinda*, etc.

ನಮ್ಮವ್ವ ಮಾತ್ರ ಇರುತ್ತಾಳೆ *S*. (ನಮ್ಮ ತಾಯಿ... *C*.)	namm'avva mâtra iruttâḷe *S*. (namma tâyi....*C*.)
Only my mother is at home	our mother only she is
ನಾವು ಬಂದೆವೆಂತ ನಿಮ್ಮವ್ವ(ನಿ)ಗೆ *S*. (ನಿಮ್ಮ ತಾಯಿಗೆ *C*.) ಹೇಳು	nâvu bandev'enta nimm'avva(ni) ge *S*. (nimma tâyige *C*.) hêḷu
Tell your mother that we are come	we came saying to your mother tell
ನಿಮ್ಮವ್ವನನ್ನು (ನಿಮ್ಮವ್ವನ್ನ) ಕರೆ	nimm'avvanannu (nimm'avvanna) kare
Call your mother	your mother call
ಬಾರೇ ಅವ್ವಾ, ಬಾಲಪ್ಪನವರು ಬಂದಿದ್ದಾರೆ	bârê[1] avvâ, bâlappanavaru band' iddâre
Come here, mother, Mr. Bâlappa is come	come mother, Bâlappa h. come they are
ಬರ್ರಿ *S*. (ಬನ್ನಿ *C*.), ಬಾಲಪ್ಪನವರೇ, ಒಳಗೆ ಬರ್ರಿ	barri *S*. (banni *C*.), bâlappanavarê, *w*oḷage barri
Come, Mr. Bâlappa, please come in	come Bâlappa in come
ಬಾಲಪ್ಪಗೆ ತುಸ ನೀರು ತಂದು ಕೊಡು	bâlappage tusa nîru tandu koḍu
Bring Mr. Bâlappa some water	to Bâlappa little water h. brought give

65. ಮಗು magu[2]=child (*G. Kind*); ಮಗ(ನು) maga (nu)=son (*G. Sohn*); ಮಗಳು magaḷu=daughter (*G. Tochter*).

Declension.

		Singular	*Plural:*
Neuter	*Nom*.	magu-v-u	makkaḷu
	Acc.	magu-v-annu	makkaḷ-annu *etc*.
	Instr.	magu-v-inda	*as* mâtugaḷu *in No. 5.*
	Dat.	magu-v-ige	
	Gen.	magu-vin-a	
	Loc.	magu-vin-alli	
Masc.		maganu declined like avanu	makkaḷu *or* magandiru
Fem.		magaḷu „ „ avaḷu	makkaḷu

[1] In calling females familiarly, the interjectional sound *ê* is added to the imperative. But strangers should not use it.

[2] *Magu* is rarely used in the Southern Mahratta country, *kûsu* is used instead.

ಇವರು ಯಾರ ಮಕ್ಕಳು?	ivaru yâra makkaḷu?
Whose are these children?	these whose children?
ಈಕೆ ನನ್ನ ಮಗಳು	îke nanna magaḷu
This is my daughter	this my daughter
ಅವರಿಬ್ಬರು ನಮ್ಮಣ್ಣನ ಮಕ್ಕಳು	avar'ibbaru namm'aṇṇana makkaḷu
Those two are my brother's children	they two our elder brother's children
ಆತ ನಮ್ಮಕ್ಕನ ಮಗ	âta namm'akkana maga
He is my sister's son (my nephew)	he our elder sister's son
ಈ ಮಗು ಎರಡನೆಯವರದು	î magu yeraḍane-y-avaradu
This child belongs to some one else	this child second theirs
ನಿಮ್ಮ ಮಕ್ಕಳಲ್ಲಿ ಚಿಕ್ಕವ ಯಾವನು?	nimma makkaḷalli čikk'ava yâvanu?
Which is the youngest of your children?	your in children little one which?
ನಿಮ್ಮ ಮಗನಿಗೆ ಈ ರೂಪಾಯಿ ಕೊಡಿರಿ	nimma maganige î rûpâyi koḍiri
Give this rupee to your son	your to son this rupee give
ನನಗೆ ಮಗನಿಲ್ಲ, ಒಬ್ಬ ಮಗಳು ಇರುತ್ತಾಳೆ	nanage magan'illa, *w*obba magaḷu iruttâḷe
I have no son, I have only a daughter	to me son is not, one daughter she is
ಹಾಗಾದರೆ ಮಗಳಿಗೆ ಕೊಡಿರಿ	hâg'âdare magaḷige koḍiri
Then give it to your daughter	so if become to daughter give
ತಾಯಿಯೂ ಮಗನೂ ಇಬ್ಬರು ಬಂದಿದ್ದಾರೆ	tâyiyû maganû ibbaru band' iddâre
Both mother and son are come	mother too son too both h. come are

66. ಇಂಥಾ inthâ = such (as this); ಅಂಥಾ anthâ[1] = such (as that) (G. *solch*); ಎಂಥಾ *y*enthâ = what kind? (G. *was für ein?*)

By adding a v a n u, a v a ḷ u (â k e), a d u (abbreviated d u or d d u), these adjectives are changed into pronouns, as, i n t h a v a n u, i n t h a v a ḷ u, i n t h â d d u = such a one as this; a n t h a v a n u, a n t h a v a ḷ u, a n t h â d d u = such a one as that; *y* e n t h a v a n u, *y* e n t h a v a ḷ u, *y* e n t h â d d u = what kind of man, woman or thing? See No. 6, Rem. 2.

ನಿಮ್ಮ ಮನೆ ಎಂಥಾದ್ದು?	nimma mane *y*enthâddu?
What sort of a house is yours?	your house what kind?

---

[1] *Anthâ* is often added to the genitive case of nouns and pronouns, or to the relative participles of verbs to give them the force of adjectives.

ನಮ್ಮ ಮನೆ ಬಹಳ ಸಣ್ಣದು
My house is very small
namma mane bahaḷa saṇṇadu
our house very small one

ಇಂಥಾ ಸಣ್ಣ ಮನೆ ನಾ ಎಂದೂ ನೋಡಿದ್ದಿಲ್ಲ
I never saw such a small house as this
inthâ saṇṇa mane nâ yendû nôḍ' idd'illa
such small house I ever h. seen h. been is not

ನಿಮ್ಮಂಥವರಿಗೆ ಇಂಥಾ ಸಣ್ಣ ಮನೆ ಯಾಕೆ?
Why should a person like you have such a small house?
nimm'anthavarige inthâ saṇṇa mane yâke?
to such as you such small house why?

ಇದು ಎಂಥಾ ಚಲೋ ಕುದುರೆ!
What a fine horse!
idu yenthâ čalô kudure!
this what kind of fine horse!

ಇಂಥಾದ್ದಕ್ಕೆ ಎಷ್ಟು ರೂಪಾಯಿ ಬೀಳುತ್ತದೆ?
What is the price of such a one?
inthâddakke yeshṭu rûpâyi bîḷuttade?
to such a one how many rupee it falls?

ನನಗೂ ಇಂಥಾದ್ದೊಂದು ಬೇಕು
I too should like to have one like this
nanagû inthâdd'ondu bêku
to me also such a one is wanted

ನೀವು ಕೊಂಡಂಥ ಕುದುರೆ ಬಹಳ ಚಲೋದು
The horse you have bought is very fine
nîvu koṇḍ'antha kudure bahaḷa čalôdu
such as you bought horse very fine one

ನೀವು ಮಾಡುವಂಥ ಕೆಲಸ ಬಹಳ
You do a great deal of work
nîvu mâḍuv' antha kelasa bahaḷa
such as you make work much

ನಮ್ಮಂಥವರಿಂದ ಅಷ್ಟು ಕೆಲಸ ಮಾಡಲಿಕ್ಕಾಗುವದಿಲ್ಲ
Our people cannot do so much
namm'anthavarinda ashṭu kelasa mâḍalikk'âguvad'illa
by such as we so much work to do the being done is not

67. ದೂರ dûra = far (*G. fern*).

ಬರ್ರಿ (ಬನ್ನಿ *C.*), ಯಾಕೆ ಅಷ್ಟು ದೂರ ನಿಂತಿರುತ್ತೀರಿ?
Come here, why are you keeping aloof
barri (banni *C.*), yâke ashṭu dûra nint' iruttîri?
come, why so far h. stood you are?

ಎಲ್ಲಿಂದ ಬಂದಿರಿ?
Where have you come from?
yellinda bandiri?
whence you came?

ನಾವು ದೂರದಿಂದ (ದೂರಿಂದ) ಬಂದೆವು
We have come from a great distance
nâvu dûradinda (dûrinda) bandevu
we from far we came

ನಮ್ಮ ಊರು ಬಹಳ ದೂರ
Our town (village) is very far
namma ûru bahaḷa dûra
our town very far

ಮುಂಬಾಯಷ್ಟು ದೂರ	**mumbây' ashṭu dûra**
As far as Bombay	of Bombay so far
ಮುಂಬಾಯಿ ಇಲ್ಲಿಗೆ (ಇಲ್ಲಿಂದೆ)ಷ್ಟು ದೂರ?	**mumbâyi illig' (illind') eshṭu dûra?**
How far is it from here to Bombay?	Bombay hither (hence) how much far?
ಇಲ್ಲಿಂದ ಮುಂಬಾಯಿಗೆ ಎಷ್ಟು ದೂರ?	**illinda mumbâyige yeshṭu dûra?**
What is the distance to Bombay?	hence to Bombay how far?
ಮುಂಬಾಯಿ (...ಗೆ) ಬಹಳ ದೂರ	**mumbâyi (...ge) bahaḷa dûra**
Bombay is very far	Bombay (to Bombay) very far
ನಿಮ್ಮ ಮಕ್ಕಳು ಎಷ್ಟೋ ದೂರ ಹೋದರು!	**nimma makkaḷu yeshṭô dûra hôdaru!**
How far away your children have gone!	your children how much far they went!
ಹೌದು, ಬಹಳ ದೂರದಲ್ಲಿರುತ್ತಾರೆ	**houdu, bahaḷa dûradall' iruttâre**
Yes, they are far away	yes, much in the distance they are

68. ಹೊತ್ತು **hottu** = time (*G. Zeit*); ಈಹೊತ್ತು **îhottu** = to-day.

ಈಹೊತ್ತು ಯಾರೂ ಬಂದಿಲ್ಲ (ಬರಲಿಲ್ಲ *C.*)	**îhottu yârû band'illa (baral'illa *C.*)**
No one is come to-day	to-day who even h. come is not (to come is not)
ಬಹಳ ಹೊತ್ತು ಮಾಡಿ ಬಂದಿರಿ	**bahaḷa hottu mâḍi bandiri**
You are very late, *or*, you have come etc.	much time h. made you came
ಹೌದಪ್ಪ, ಹೊತ್ತಾಯಿತು	**houd'appa hott' âyitu**
Yes, sir, it is late	yes father, time became
ಎಷ್ಟೊತ್ತಾಯಿತು?	**yesht' hott' âyitu?**
What is the time? *or* what time is it?	how much time it became?
ಬಹಳ ಹೊತ್ತಾಯಿತು, ಏಳು ಘಂಟೆ ಆಗಿ ಹೋಯಿತು	**bahaḷa hott'âyitu, yêḷu ghaṇṭe âgi hôyitu**
It is very late, it is past seven	much time it became, seven bell h. become it went
ಎರಡೂ ಹೊತ್ತು ಕೆಲಸ ಮಾಡ ಬೇಕು	**yeradû hottu kelasa mâḍa bêku**
You are to work morning and afternoon	two even time work to do is wanted

ಒಪ್ಪತ್ತು ಕೆಲಸ ಮಾಡುತ್ತೇವೆ	*w*oppattu[1] kelasa mâḍuttêve
We shall work half a day only	one time work we do
ಹೊತ್ಹೋಯಿತು, ಮನೆಗೆ ಹೋಗಿರಿ	hott' hôyitu, manege hôgiri
It is evening, go home now	time went, to house go
ಬಂದು ಈಹೊತ್ತಿಗೆಷ್ಟುದಿವಸವಾಯಿತು? *or* ಈಹೊತ್ತಿಗೆಷ್ಟುದಿವಸವಾಯಿತು ಬಂದು?	bandu îhottig'eshṭu divasa-v-âyitu? *or* ihottig'eshṭu divasa-v-âyitu bandu?
How long is it since you came?	this time how many day it became h. come?
ಮೂರು ದಿವಸದ ಮೇಲೆ ಒಪ್ಪತ್ತು ಕೆಲಸ ಮಾಡಿದ್ದೇವೆ	mûru divasada mêle *w*oppattu kelasa maḍ'iddêve
We have worked for three days and a half	above three day one time work h. done we are

69. ದಿವಸ divasa = day (*G. Tag*).

Instead of divasa, ದಿನ dina is also much used.

ಯಾವ ದಿವಸ ಬಂದಿರಿ?	yâva divasa bandiri?
What day did you arrive?	whaṭ day you came?
ಈಹೊತ್ತಿನ ದಿವಸ ಬಂದೆ	îhottina divasa[2] bande
I have come to-day	of to-day day I came
ಎರಡು ದಿವಸದ ಮೇಲೆ ಹೋಗುತ್ತೇನೆ	*y*eraḍu divasada mêle hôguttène
I am going away after two days	two of day after I go
ಇನ್ನೂ ನಾಲ್ಕು ದಿವಸ ಇದ್ದು ಹೋಗಿರಿ	innû nâlku[3] divasa iddu hôgiri
Stay a few days more	still even four day h. been go
ಈ ಅಕ್ಕಿ ಎಷ್ಟು ದಿವಸ ಸಾಕಾಗುತ್ತದೆ?	î akki *y*eshṭu divasa sâkâguttade?
How many days will this rice last?	this rice how many day it suffice?
ಎಂಟು ದಿವಸದ ತನಕ ಸಾಕಾದೀತು	*y*enṭu divasada tanaka sâkâdîtu
It will last for a week	eight day's till it will suffice
ಈ ಗಾಡಿ ಎಷ್ಟು ದಿವಸದಲ್ಲಿ ಮಾಡಬಹುದು?	î gâḍi *y*eshṭu divasadalli mâḍa bahudu?
Within how many days can you make this coach?	this coach how many in day to make it will come?

---

1 The Old Kanarese words ಒರ್ *wor* = *wondu*, and ಪೊೞ್ತು *portu* = *hottu*, when joined together, become "*worportu*". and this has baen changed into *woppattu* = half a day.

2 The crude form instead of the locative case.

3 *Nâlku divasa* is often used in the sense of "some days, a few days".

ಹದಿನೈದು ದಿವಸದೊಳಗೆ ಮಾಡಿ ಕೊಡುತ್ತೇನೆ	hadineidu divasad'oḷage mâḍi koḍuttêne
I shall finish it within a fortnight	fifteen of day within h. made I give
ದಿನ ದಿನ ಅದೇ ಮಾತು ಹೇಳುತ್ತೀರಿ	dina dina adê mâtu hêḷuttîri
You say the same every day	day day *that* word you say
ನಾವೇನು? ನಾಲ್ಕು ದಿವಸದವರು	nâv'ênu? nâlku[1] divasad'avaru
What are we? we are very short lived	we what? four of day they

70. ರಾತ್ರಿ râtri = night (*G. Nacht*).

ರಾತ್ರಿ ಆಯಿತು	râtri âyitu
It has grown dark; it is night	night it became
ಎಷ್ಟು ರಾತ್ರಿ?	*y*eshṭu râtri?
What time of the night?	how much night?
ಬಹಳ ರಾತ್ರಿ ಆಯಿತು [in the night	bahaḷa râtri âyitu
It is very dark; *or*, it is very late	much night it became
ಆರು ತಾಸು ರಾತ್ರಿ	âru tâsu râtri
(It is) midnight	six hour night
ಬಹಳ ರಾತ್ರಿ ಮಾಡಿ ಬಂದಿರಿ	bahaḷa râtri mâḍi bandiri
How late you came!	much night h. made you came
ರಾತ್ರೀ ಹೊತ್ತಿನಲ್ಲಿ (ರಾತ್ರಿಯಲ್ಲಿ) ಬರ ಬಾರದಿತ್ತು	râtrî[2] hottinalli (râtriyalli) bara bârad'ittu
You ought not to have come at night	night in the time (at night) to come the not coming was
ಈ ರಾತ್ರಿ ನಮ್ಮ ತಮ್ಮ ಬರುತ್ತಾನೆ	î râtri namma tamma baruttâne
To-night my brother is coming	this night our younger brother comes
ದಿನಾ ರಾತ್ರಿ ನಮ್ಮ ಮನೆಗೆ ಬರುತ್ತಾನೆ	dinâ râtri[3] namma manege baruttâne
He comes to our house every night	of day night our to house he comes
ರಾತ್ರಿಯೆಲ್ಲಾ ಏನು ಮಾಡುತ್ತಾನೆ?	râtri-y-ellâ *y*ênu mâḍuttâne?
What does he do all night? what is he doing...?	night all what he does?
ರಾತ್ರಿಯೆಲ್ಲಾ ಮಲಗಿಕೊಂಡಿರುತ್ತಾನೆ	râtri-y-ellâ malagikoṇḍ' iruttâne
He sleeps the whole night	night all h. lain down he is

[1] *Nâlku divasa* is often used in the sense of "some days, a few days".
[2] *Râtrî*=*râtriya* = of the night.
[3] *Dinâ*, instead of *dinada; dinâ râtri* = every day at night.

71. ಹಗಲು hagalu = day, day-time (*G. Tag*).

ರಾತ್ರೀ ಬರ ಬೇಡ, ಹಗಲ ಹೊತ್ತು ಬಾ	**râtrî bara bêḍa, hagala[1] hottu bâ**
Come in the day-time, not at night	of night to come not wanted, of day-time come
ರಾತ್ರಿ ಹೋಗಿ ಹಗಲಾಯಿತು	**râtri hôgi hagal' âyitu**
Night has past and day has come	night h. gone day it became
ಹಗಲೆಲ್ಲಾ ಏನು ಮಾಡಿದಿ?	**hagal'ellâ yênu mâḍidi?**
What have you been doing all day?	day all what thou didst?
ಹಗಲೆಲ್ಲಾ ಕೆಲಸದಲ್ಲಿದ್ದೆ	**hagal'ellâ kelasadall' idde**
I have been engaged the whole day	day all in work I was
ಹಗಲೆಲ್ಲಾ ನಮ್ಮ ಮನೆಗೆ ಬರುತ್ತಿರುತ್ತಾನೆ	**hagal'ellâ namma manege barutt' irut'tâne**
He continually freqnents our house	day all our to house coming he is
ರಾತ್ರೀ ಹಗಲೂ ಬರಕೋತ ಕೂತಿರುತ್ತಾನೆ	**râtrî hagalû bara[2]kôta[3]kût'[4]iru-ttâne**
He is writing day and night	night day even writing h. sat he is
ಹಗಲ ಹೊತ್ತು ಕೆಲಸ ಮಾಡಿ ರಾತ್ರೀ ಮಲಗಿಕೋ	**hagala hottu kelasa mâḍi, râtrî malagikô**
Work in the day-time, and sleep at night	of day-time work h. done, at night lie down
ಹಗಲಿಗೆ ಹನ್ನೆರಡು ತಾಸು	**hagalige hanneraḍu tâsu**
A day has twelve hours	to the day-time twelve hour
ಮೂರು ದಿವಸ ಹಗಲೂ ರಾತ್ರೀ ಮಲಗಿಕೊಳ್ಳಲಿಲ್ಲ	**mûru divasa hagalû râtrî malagi-koḷḷal'illa**
I have not been in bed for three days and nights	three day even night the lying down is not

72. ಬಿಸಿಲು bisilu[5] = sunshine, heat of the sun (*G. Sonnenschein*).

ಈ ಹೊತ್ತು ಎಷ್ಟೋ ಬಿಸಿಲದೆ!	**î hottu yeshṭô bisil'ade!**
How hot it is to-day!	this time how much heat is!
ಹೌದು, ಬಹಳ ಬಿಸಿಲು ಬಿದ್ದದೆ	**houdu, bahaḷa bisilu bidd' ade**
Yes, it is very hot	yes, much heat h. fallen is

---

[1] *Hagala*, instead of *hagalina* = of the day.
[2] Instead of *baradu*.
[3] *Kôta*, a colloquial abbreviation for *koḷḷutta*.
[4] *Kûtu*.
[5] Instead of *bisilu*, *bisalu* is common in S. M.

ಈಗ ಬಿಸಿಲಿನ ದಿವಸ	**îga bisilina divasa**
Now is the hot season	now of heat day
ಈಹೊತ್ತಿನಷ್ಟು ಬಿಸಿಲು ನಾ ಎಂದೂ ನೋಡಿದ್ದಿಲ್ಲ	**î hottin'ashṭu bisilu nâ yendû nôḍ'idd'illa**
I have never seen so hot a day as this	to-day's as much heat I never h. seen h. been
ಇಲ್ಲಿ ಅಲ್ಲಿ ಬಿಸಿಲುಕುದುರೆ ಕಾಣುತ್ತದೆ	**illi alli bisilukudure kâṇuttade**
Mirages may be seen here and there	here there heat-horse it appears
ಬಿಸಿಲಿಗೆ ಹೋಗಬೇಡ	**bisilige hôga bêḍa**
Do not expose yourself to the sun	within heat to go is not wanted
ಬಿಸಿಲಿನಲ್ಲಿ ಯಾರು ಕೆಲಸ ಮಾಡ್ಯಾರು!	**bisilinalli yâru kelasa mâḍyâru!**
Who can work in the sun!	in heat who work they may do!
ಇದು ಯಾತರ ಬಿಸಿಲು!	**idu yâtara bisilu!**
What heat is this! *i. e.* this heat is not great	this of which heat
ಇದು ಬಿಸಿಲಲ್ಲ	**idu bisil' alla**
This cannot be called heat	this heat not
ಈ ಅಕ್ಕಿ ಬಿಸಿಲಿಗೆ ಹಾಕು	**î akki bisilige hâku**
Put this rice out in the sun	this rice to heat place

73. ಗೊತ್ತು **gottu** = certainty, knowledge, acquaintance

(G. Gewissheit, Bekanntschaft).

ಕುದುರೆ ಗೊತ್ತುಮಾಡಿದರೋ?	**kudure gottu maḍidar'ô?**
Has an arrangement about a horse been made?	horse certainty they made?
ಗೊತ್ತು ಮಾಡಿದರೋ ಇಲ್ಲೋ ನನಗೆ ಗೊತ್ತಿಲ್ಲ	**gottu mâḍidar'ô ill'ô nanage gott' illa**
I do not know whether it has been made or not	certainty they made? what? to me knowledge is not
ಯಾರಿಗೆ ಗೊತ್ತು?	**yârige gottu?**
Who knows?	to whom knowledge?
ನಿನಗೆ ಗೊತ್ತಾದರೆ ಹೇಳು	**ninage gott' âdare hêḷu**
Tell me if you know	to thee knowledge if become tell

ಗೊತ್ತಿಲ್ಲದ ಮಾತು ಹೇಳ ಬೇಡ	gott' illada mâtu hêḷa bêḍa
Do not say things of which you are not sure	which is not certainty word to say is not wanted
ಈ ಹುಡುಗಿಯನ್ನು ಗೊತ್ತಿಗೆ ತರಬೇಕು	i huḍugiyannu gottige tara bêku
Something should be settled about this girl; *or*, this girl should be married	this girl to certainty to bring is wanted
ಯಾರಿಗೆ ಗೊತ್ತು ಮಾಡಲಿ?	yârige gottu mâḍali?
To whom should she be betrothed?	to whom certainty let (*a. p.*) make?
ಗೊತ್ತಿನವರಲ್ಲಿ ನೋಡ ಬೇಕು	gottin' avaralli nôḍa bêku
We must look for some one among our acquaintances	among people of acquaintance to look is wanted
ಆಗಲೇ ಗೊತ್ತಾಯಿತು	âgalê gott' âyitu
She is already betrothed; *or*, it is already settled; *or*, it is already known	*then* certainty it became
ಹಾಗಾದರೆ ಒಂದು ದಿವಸ ಗೊತ್ತು ಮಾಡೋಣ	hâg'âdare *w*ondu divasa gottu mâḍôṇa
Then let us fix a day	thus if become one day certainty let us make

74. ಉಂಟು uṇṭu = there is, there are; existence (*G. ist, sind, es gibt; Dasein*).

Uṇṭu is 3rd person singular of the old root uḷ = to be; it is likewise used as a noun in the sense of existence, being. It is rarely used in Southern Mahratta, except as a noun in the phrase uṇṭu mâḍu = to create, but very extensively on the Coast and in Mysore. The relative participle of this root is uḷḷa = being, having, which is often added to nouns, to give them the force of adjectives, in the same way as the English affix *ful* in "powerful" and the like; *e. g.* bala = power; bala-v-uḷḷa = power being = having power = powerful.

ನಿಮಗೆ ಕುದುರೆ ಉಂಟೋ? *C.*	nimage kudure uṇṭô? *C.*
Have you got a horse?	to you horse there is?
ಉಂಟು *C.*	uṇṭu *C.*
Yes	there is
ಮೂರು ಕುದುರೆಗಳುಂಟು	mûru kuduregaḷ'uṇṭu
I have got three horses	three horses there are

ರೂಪಾಯಿ ಉಂಟಾದವನು ಕುದುರೆ ಇಟ್ಟುಕೊಳ್ಳ ಬಹುದು *C.* (ರೂಪಾಯಿ ಇದ್ದವನು...*S.*)	rûpâyi uṇṭ'âd'avanu kudure iṭṭukoḷḷa bahudu *C.* (rûpâyi iddavanu...*S.*)
He who has money may keep [horses	rupee he who has got horse to keep can (rupee he who had...)
ಇವರಿಗೆ ಬಹಳ ರೂಪಾಯಿ ಉಂಟು *C.* (...ರೂಪಾಯಿಗಳವೆ *S.*)	ivarige bahaḷa rûpâyi uṇṭu *C.* (...rûpâyigaḷ'ave *S.*)
This person (*or plural*) has plenty of money	to these much rupee there is (rupees are)
ಅವನಿಗೆ ಐದು ಮಂದಿ ಮಕ್ಕಳುಂಟು *C.* (...ಅವೆ *S.*)	avanige eidu mandi makkaḷ'uṇṭu *C.* (...ave *S.*)
He has five children	to him five persons children there are
ತನಗೆ ಉಂಟಾದದ್ದೆಲ್ಲಾ (ಇದ್ದದ್ದನ್ನೆಲ್ಲಾ *S.*) ಮಕ್ಕಳಿಗೆ ಕೊಟ್ಟನು *C.*	tanage uṇṭ'âdadd'ellâ (iddaddann' ellâ *S.*) makkaḷige koṭṭanu *C.*
He gave all his property to his children	to himself the being (the h. become) all to children he gave
ಎಲ್ಲಾ ಉಂಟು ಮಾಡಿದವರ್ಯಾರು?	*y*ellâ uṇṭu mâḍid'avar'yâru?
Who made all things?	all they that created who?
ನಮಗೆ ಕಾಣುವಂಥಾದ್ದೆಲ್ಲಾ ಹ್ಯಾಗೆ ಉಂಟಾಯಿತು?	namage kâṇuv' anthâdd'ellâ hyâge uṇṭ'âyitu?
How did all things that we see come into existence?	to us such thing as appears all how it was created?
ಅಂಥಾ ಮಾತು ಆಗುವದುಂಟೇ?	anthâ mâtu âguvad' uṇṭê?
Is such a thing possible?	such word the becoming is there?

75. ಕೆಡು keḍu *or* ಕೆಟ್ಟೋಗು keṭṭ'hôgu = to become bad, ...rotten (*G. schlecht werden*).

ಈ ಅನ್ನವೆಲ್ಲಾ ಕೆಟ್ಟೋಯಿತು	î anna-v-ellâ keṭṭ'hôyitu
This rice has all become stale	this c. rice all has become bad
ಅದನ್ನುಂಡರೆ ಬಾಯಿ ಕೆಡುತ್ತದೆ	adann'uṇḍare bâyi keḍuttade
If you eat it, you will lose your appetite	that if eaten mouth it becomes bad
ಅದು ಕೆಡುವದು ಹ್ಯಾಗೆ?	adu keḍuvadu hyâge?
How can it become stale?	that the becoming bad how?
ಇದನ್ನು ಯಾಕೆ ಕೆಡಿಸಿದಿ?	idannu yâke keḍisidi?
Why have you spoiled this?	this why thou spoiledst?

ಕೆಡದ ಹಾಗೆ ನೋಡ ಬೇಕು
keḍada hâge nôḍa bêku

See that it be not spoiled
not becoming bad like to see is wanted

ಬಹಳ ಹೊತ್ತು ನಿಂತು ಕೆಟ್ಟಿತು
bahaḷa hottu nintu keṭṭitu

It has become stale by standing for a long time
much time h. stood it became bad

ಈ ನೀರೂ ಬಹಳ ಕೆಟ್ಟದ್ದು
î nîrû bahaḷa keṭṭaddu[1]

This water is also very bad
this water also very bad

ಹೌದು, ಇದು ಬಹಳ ಕೆಟ್ಟ ನೀರು
houdu, idu bahaḷa keṭṭa nîru

Yes, this water is very bad
yes, this very bad water

ನೀರು ಕೆಟ್ಟರೆ, ಊರೂ ಕೆಡ ಬೇಕೇ?
nîru keṭṭare, ûrû keḍa bêkê?

If the water become bad, why should the town become so too?
water if become bad, town too to become bad is wanted?

ಈ ಊರಿನವರು ಕೆಟ್ಟೋಗಿದ್ದಾರೆ
î ûrin' avaru keṭṭ' hôg' iddâre

The people of this town have degenerated
this of town they have become bad

76. ಇಡು **iḍu**=to put, to place (*G. setzen, legen, stellen*). See No. 41; ಇಟ್ಟುಕೊಳ್ಳು **iṭṭukoḷḷu**=to keep (*G. behalten, aufbewahren*).

ಈ ಅನ್ನ ತೆಗೆದಿಡು
î anna teged' iḍu

Take this rice away
this c. rice h. taken put

ಅದನ್ನು ಮುಚ್ಚಿಡು
adannu mučč' iḍu

Keep it covered up
that h. shut put

ಮುಚ್ಚಿಡುತ್ತೇನೆ
mučč' iḍuttêne

I shall cover it up
h. shut I put

ಎಲ್ಲಿಡಲಿ?
yell' iḍali?

Where shall I put it?
where let (*a. p.*) put?

ಎಲ್ಲಿಯಾದರೂ ಇಟ್ಟು ಬಿಡು
yelli-y-âdarû iṭṭu biḍu

Put it down somewhere
where if become even h. put leave

ಕುದುರೆಯ ಮುಂದೆ ಇಟ್ಟು ಬಾ
kudureya munde iṭṭu bâ

Give it to the horse and come back
horse's before h. put come

ಈ ಕುದುರೆ ಇಟ್ಟುಕೊಳ್ಳುತ್ತೀರೋ? *C.* (...ರೇನು? *S.*)
î kudure iṭṭukoḷḷuttîrô? *C.* (-rênu? *S.*)

Are you going to keep this horse?
this horse you keep? (what?)

---

[1] *Keṭṭaddu* = that which has become bad, a bad one; see note 1, p. 21.

ಇಟ್ಟುಕೊಳ್ಳುತ್ತೇನೆ	**iṭṭukoḷḷuttêne**
Yes, I shall keep it	I keep
ಈಕೆಯ ಮೇಲೆ ಯಾಕೆ ಕಣ್ಣಿಡುತ್ತಾನೆ?	**îkeya mêle yâke kaṇṇ'iḍuttâne?**
Why is he gazing on her?	her on why eye he puts??
ಆಕೆಯನ್ನು ಇಟ್ಟುಕೊಳ್ಳ ಬೇಕೆಂದಿರುತ್ತಾನೋ?	**âkeyannu iṭṭukoḷḷa bêk'end'iru? ttân'ô?**
Does he want to take her as his concubine?	her to keep is wanted h. said he is?

77. ತೋರು **tôru**=to appear, to seem (*G. scheinen, erscheinen*); ತೋರಿಸು **tôrisu**=to show (*G. zeigen*).

ಈ ಮಾತು ನಿಮಗೆ ಹ್ಯಾಗೆ ತೋರುತ್ತದೆ?	**î mâtu nimage hyâge tôruttade?**
What do you think of this matter?	this word to you how it appears?
ನಿಮಗೆ ತೋರಿದ ಹಾಗೆ ಹೇಳಿರಿ	**nimage tôrida hâge hêḷiri**
Tell me what you think of it; *or*, tell me how it appears to you	to you as it appeared tell
ನಿಮಗೆ ತೋರುವ ಹಾಗೆ ನನಗೆ ತೋರುವದಿಲ್ಲ	**nimage tôruva hâge nanage tôru-vad'illa**
My opinion differs from yours; *or*, I do not see it as you do	to you appearing like to me the appearing is not
ಇದು ರೂಪಾಯಿಯ ಹಾಗೆ ತೋರುತ್ತದಲ್ಲಾ?	**idu rupâyiya hâge tôruttad'allâ?**
Does not this look like a rupee?	this rupee's like it seems not?
ಹೀಗೆ ತೋರುತ್ತದೆ	**hîge tôruttade**
So it looks, so it seems	so it seems
ಇವರಿಗೆ ನಿಮ್ಮ ಮನೆ ತೋರಿಸು	**ivarige nimma mane tôrisu**
Show him your house	to them your house show [*C.*)
ಮನೆ ತೋರಿಸುತ್ತೇನೆ, ಬರ್ರಿ *S.* (..ಬನ್ನಿ *C.*)	**mane tôrisuttêne, barri** *S.* (**...banni**
Come along, I will show you my house	house I show, come
ಮನೆ ತೋರಿಸುತ್ತಾನಂತೆ, ಹೋಗಿರಿ	**mane tôrisuttân' ante, hôgiri**
Go, he says he will show you his house	house he shows it says, go
ಈ ಕೆಲಸ ನನಗೆ ತೋರಿಸಿ ಕೊಡಿರಿ	**î kelasa nanage tôrisi koḍiri**
Teach me how to do this job	this work to me h. shown give
ನಿಮಗೆ ತೋರಿದ ಹಾಗೆ ಮಾಡಿರಿ	**nimage tôrida hâge mâḍiri**
Do as you think best	to you appeared like do

78. ಉಣ್ಣು uṇṇu, ತಿನ್ನು tinnu = to eat (*G. essen*); ಊಟ ûṭa = Meal (*G. das Essen*).

ಊಟಾಯಿತೋ?	uṭ' âyit'ô?
Is dinner (or supper) over?	meal it is done?
ಇನ್ನೂ ಆಗಲಿಲ್ಲ	innû âgal' illa
Not yet	yet even to be done is not
ಉಂಡು ಬಂದೆ, *or* ಊಟ ಮಾಡಿ ಬಂದೆ	uṇḍu bande, *or* ûṭa mâḍi bande
I have dined (supped)	h. eaten I came, meal h. made I came
ಉಂಡು ಬಹಳ ಹೊತ್ತಾಯಿತು	uṇḍu bahaḷa hott'âyitu
I dined long ago	h. eaten much time became
ಈಗ ಊಟಕ್ಕೆ (*or* ಉಣ್ಣಲಿಕ್ಕೆ) ಹೋಗುತ್ತೇನೆ	îga ûṭakke (*or* uṇṇalikke) hôguttêne
I am now going to take my meal	now to meal (to eat) I go
ಅನ್ನಾ ಉಣ್ಣುತ್ತೀರೋ? *C.*...ಉಣ್ಣುತ್ತೀರೇನು? *S.*	annâ uṇṇuttîrô? *C.*...uṇṇuttîr'ênu? *S.*
Do you eat rice?	c. rice you eat? ...you eat what?
ಉಣ್ಣುತ್ತೇನೆ	uṇṇuttêne
Yes	I eat
ಹಾಗಾದರೆ ಊಟಮಾಡಿ ಬರ್ರಿ *S.* (ಬನ್ನಿ *C.*)	hâg'âdare ûṭa mâḍi barri *S.* (banni *C.*)
Then go to dinner	so if become meal h. made come
ಉಣ್ಣಿರಿ, ಉಣ್ಣದೆ ಕೆಲಸ ಮಾಡಲಾರಿರಿ	uṇṇiri, uṇṇade kelasa mâdal' âriri
Eat, you cannot work unless you eat	eat, not h. eaten work to do you cannot
ಉಣ್ಣಲಾರೆ, *or* ಊಟ ಮಾಡಲಾರೆ	uṇṇal' âre, *or* ûṭa mâḍal' âre
I cannot eat	to eat I. cannot, meal to make I cannot

79. *The same continued*

ಮೂರು ದಿವಸದಿಂದ ಉಣ್ಣಲಿಲ್ಲ, *or* ...ಉಂಡಿಲ್ಲ	mûru divasadinda uṇṇal'illa *or* ...uṇḍ'illa
I have not eaten anything for three days	three from day to eat is not, h. eaten I am not
ಏನೂ ಉಣ್ಣದೆ ಹಾಗೇ ಮಲಗಿಕೊಂಡೆ	yênû uṇṇade hâgê malagikoṇḍe
I lay down without eating anything	what even not h. eaten *so* I lay down

ಉಂಡದ್ದು ಉಂಡ ಹಾಗೆ ಹೋಗುತ್ತದೆ	uṇḍaddu uṇḍa hâge hôguttade
What I eat goes off undigested	the eaten (thing) as eaten it goes
ಉಂಡು ಉಂಡು ಸಾಕಾಯಿತು	uṇḍu uṇḍu sâk' âyitu
I have quite enough of it	h. eaten h. eaten enough it became
ಉಂಡ ಮೇಲೆ ಬಾ, *or* ಊಟಾದ ಮೇಲೆ ಬಾ	uṇḍa mêle bâ *or* ûṭ'âda mêle bâ
Come after dinner (supper)	after eating come, after meal being [done come
ಈ ಹೂವು ಯಾಕೆ ತಿನ್ನುತ್ತೀ?	î hûvu yâke tinnuttî?
Why are you eating this flower?	this flower why thou eatest?
ಇದು ತಿನ್ನಲಿಕ್ಕೆ ಬರುವದಿಲ್ಲ	idu tinnalikke baruvad' illa
This cannot be eaten,... is not eatable	this to eat the coming is not
ಎಲ್ಲಾ ತಿಂದುಬಿಟ್ಟಿ	yellâ tindu biṭṭi
You have eaten it all; *or* you have eaten up everything	all h. eaten thou leftst
ತಿನ್ನ ಬಾರದಿತ್ತು	tinna bârad' ittu[1]
You should not have eaten it	to eat the not coming was
ಇದು ತಿನ್ನುವಂಥಾದ್ದಲ್ಲ	idu tinnuv'anthâdd' alla
This is not eatable	this eating such one not

80. ಅನ್ನ. anna = cooked rice, food (*G. gekochter Reis, Speise*).

ಇಲ್ಲಿ ಅಕ್ಕಿ ಅವೆ, ಅನ್ನ ಮಾಡು	illi akki ave[2], anna mâḍu
Here is rice, cook it	here rice is, c. rice make
ಅನ್ನ ಇನ್ನೂ ಆಗಲಿಲ್ಲೇನು? *S.* ...(ಇನ್ನೂ ಆಗಲಿಲ್ಲವೋ? *C.*)	anna innû âgal' ill'ênu? *S.* (... innû âgal'illavô? *C.*)
Is the rice not yet ready?	c. rice yet even to become is not what? [(... is not?)
ಅನ್ನವಾಯಿತು, ಬರ್ರಿ *S.*(...ಬನ್ನಿ *C.*)	anna-v-âyitu, barri *S.* (banni *C.*)
The rice is ready, come (to dinner)	it became c. rice, come (come)
ಈ ಅನ್ನ ಚಲೋದಲ್ಲ *S.*(...ಒಳ್ಳೇದಲ್ಲ *C.*)	î anna čalôd' alla *S.* (...*wo*ḷḷêd' alla *C.*)
This rice is not nice	this c. rice nice not (good not)
ಈ ಅನ್ನದಲ್ಲೇನದೆ?	î annadall'ên' ade?
What is there in this rice?	this in c. rice what is?

[1] Instead of *bâradd'ittu*, verbal noun of the negative form.

[2] *Akki* is generally considered as a collective noun and followed by a verb in the plural.

ಈ ಅನ್ನಾ ಏನು ಮಾಡಿದಿ?	î annâ *y*ênu mâḍidi?
What have you done with this rice?	this c. rice what thou madest?
ಈ ಅನ್ನ ನನಗೆ ಹೋಗುವದಿಲ್ಲ	î anna nanage hôguvad' illa
I cannot eat this rice	this c. rice to me the going is not
ಈ ಅನ್ನಾ ಆ ಹುಡುಗರಿಗೆ ಉಣ್ಣಿಸು	î annâ â huḍugarige uṇṇisu
Give this rice to those children to eat	this c. rice those to boys make eat
ನಿಮ್ಮನ್ನಾ ಉಣ್ಣುತ್ತೇನೆ	nimm'annâ uṇṇuttêne
I am supported by you	your c. rice I eat
ನನಗೆ ಅನ್ನಾ ಹಾಕುವವರು ನೀವೇ	nanage annâ hâkuv' avaru nîvê
You are my supporter	to me c. rice throwing they *you*

81. ಕಿವಿ kivi = ear (*G. Ohr*).

ನಿನಗೆ ಕಿವಿ ಎಷ್ಟು? *or* . . . ಎಷ್ಟು ಕಿವಿ?	ninage kivi *y*eshṭu? *or* .. *y*eshṭu kivi?
How many ears have you?	to you ear how many?
ನನಗೆ ಎರಡು ಕಿವಿ	nanage *y*eraḍu kivi
I have two ears	to me two ear
ಹಾಗಾದರೆ ಯಾಕೆ ಕಿವಿಗೊಡುವದಿಲ್ಲ?	hâg' âdare *y*âke kivigoḍuvad'illa?[1]
Then why are you not listening?	thus if become why ear the giving is not?
ಕಿವಿಗೊಟ್ಟು ಕೇಳು	kivi goṭṭu kêḷu
Listen attentively; *or*, pay attention	ear h. given hear
ಕಿವಿ ಮುಚ್ಚಿ ಕೊಳ್ಳ ಬೇಡ	kivi mučči koḷḷa bêḍa
Do not shut your ears	ear h. shut to take is not wanted
ಈ ಮಾತು ಅವನ ಕಿವಿಯ ಮೇಲೆ ಹಾಕಿದ	î mâtu avana kiviya mêle hâkida
He mentioned this matter to him	this word his ear's on he threw
ಕಿವಿಯಿಂದ ಕೇಳುತ್ತೇವೆ	kiviyinda kêluttêve
We hear with our ears	with (the) ear we hear
ನನ್ನದೊಂದು ಕಿವಿ ಕೇಳುವದಿಲ್ಲ	nannad'ondu kivi kêḷuvad' illa
I am deaf on one ear	mine one ear the hearing is not
ಈ ಕಿವಿಯಿಂದ ಏನೂ ಕೇಳಲಾರೆ	î kiviyinda *y*ênu kêḷal'âre
I cannot hear anything on this ear	this with ear what even to hear I cannot
ಕಿವಿಮಾತು	kivimâtu
A whisper	ear-word

1 Instead of *kivi koḍuvad'illa.*

82. ಕಾಲು kâlu = leg, foot (*G. Bein, Fuss*).

ನಮಗೆರಡು ಕಾಲವೆ	**namag'eraḍu kâl'ave**
We have two legs	to us two leg they are
ಕುದುರೆಗೆ ನಾಲ್ಕು ಕಾಲು	**kuduregе nâlku kâlu**
A horse has four legs	to the horse four leg
ಮುಂಗಾಲು ಎರಡು, ಹಿಂಗಾಲು ಎರಡು	**muṅ'gâlu[1] *y*eraḍu, hiṅ'gâlu[1] *y*eraḍu**
Two fore and two hind legs	fore leg two, hind leg two
ಇವನಿಗೆ ಕಾಲಿಲ್ಲ, ನೋಡು	**ivanige kâl'ila, nôḍu**
Look, this man is lame	to him leg is not, see
ನಿಮ್ಮ ಕಾಲಿಗೇನಾಗಿದಪ್ಪಾ?	**nimma kâlig'ên' âg' id' appâ?**
What is the matter with your legs, sir?	your to leg what h. become it is father?
ಚಿಕ್ಕಂದಿನಿಂದ ಕೈಕಾಲು ಹೋಗಿವೆ	**čikk'andininda keikâlu hôg'ive**
My hands and feet have been crippled from my childhood	small from that time hand foot are gone
ಕಾಲಿನ ಮೇಲೆ ಬೆಂಕಿ ಬಿದ್ದು ಹೀಗಾಯಿತು	**kâlina mêle beṅki biddu hîg' âyitu**
It was caused by fire falling on my legs	of the leg on fire h. fallen like this it became
ಕಾಲ್ಬೀಳುತ್ತೇನೆ, ಏನಾದರೂ ಕೊಡಿರಿ	**kâl'bîḷuttêne[2], *y*ên'âdarû koḍiri**
I implore you on my knees to give me something	foot I fall, what if become even give
ನಿಮ್ಮ ಮಗನಿಗೆ ಕಾಲು ಬಂದದೋ? *C.* (...ಬಂದದೇನು? *S.*)	**nimma maganige kâlu band'adô?** *C.* (...**band'ad'ênu?** *S.*)
Can your son already walk?	your to son foot h. come is? (...what?)
ಬಂದದೆ	**band' ade**
Yes, he can	h. come it is

83. ಪಾಠ pâṭha = lesson (*G. Lektion, Aufgabe*).

ನಿಮಗೆ ಎಷ್ಟು ಪಾಠ ಬರುತ್ತವೆ?	**nimage *y*eshṭu pâṭha baruttave?**
How many lessons do you know?	to you how many lesson they come?
ನೂರು ಪಾಠ ಓದಿದ್ದೇವೆ	**nûru pâṭha *w*ôd' iddêve**
We have read one hundred lessons	100 lesson h. read we are

---

[1] Instead of ***mundina kâlu, hindina kâlu.***

[2] Instead of ***kâlige bîḷuttêne*** = I fall to (your) feet.

ಒಂದನೇ ಪಾಠದಿಂದ ನೂರರ ತನಕ	*w*ondane pâṭhadinda nûrara tanaka
From the first to the 100th lesson	first from lesson of hundred as far
ನೂರನೇ ಪಾಠದಿಂದ ಮುಂದೆ ಓದಲಿಲ್ಲ	nûranê pâṭhadinda munde *w*ôdal'illa
We have not read beyond the 100th lesson	100th from lesson forward to read is not
ಬಾಯಿಪಾಠ ಮಾಡಿದಿರೋ? *C.* ...ಮಾಡಿದಿರೇನು? *S.*	bâyipâṭha mâḍidirô? *C* ...mâḍidir'-ênu? *S.*
Did you learn them by heart?	mouth-lesson did you make? you [made what?
ಕೆಲವು ಪಾಠ ಮಾಡಿದೆವು	kelavu pâṭha mâḍidevu
We learnt some	some lesson we made
ನಾಲ್ಕೈದು ಬಾಯಿಪಾಠ ಬರುತ್ತವೆ	nâlk'eidu bâyipâṭha baruttave
We know four or five by heart	four five mouth-lesson they come
ಪಾಠ ಮಾಡಲಿಕ್ಕೆ ಎಷ್ಟು ದಿವಸ ಬೇಕಾದವು?	pâṭha mâḍalikke *y*eshṭu divasa bêk'-âdavu?
How many days did it take you to learn them?	lesson to make how many day were wanted? [divasa
ಒಂದೊಂದು ಪಾಠಕ್ಕೆ ಒಂದೊಂದು ದಿವಸ	*w*ond'ondu pâṭhakke *w*ond' ondu
One day for each lesson	one one to lesson one one day
ಹತ್ತನೇ ಪಾಠಕ್ಕೆ ಎರಡು ದಿವಸ	hattanê pâṭhakke *y*eraḍu divasa
For the tenth lesson two days	tenth to lesson two day

84. ಆಡು **âḍu** = to play (*G. spielen*); ಆಟ **âṭa** = play, game (*G. Spiel*); ಮಾತಾಡು **mâtâḍu** = to speak, to talk (*G. sprechen*).

ಈ ಹುಡುಗರು ಏನಾಡುತ್ತಾರೆ?	î huḍugaru *y*ên' âḍuttâre?
What are these boys playing?	these boys what they play?
ಅವರನ್ನು ಮಾತಾಡಿಸಿ ಕೇಳು	avarannu mâtâḍisi kêḷu
Speak to them and ask them	them h. made to talk ask
ಅವರು ಮಾತಾಡುವದಿಲ್ಲ	avaru mâtâḍuvad' illa
They won't speak	they the talking is not
ಆಡ ಬಾ ಅನ್ನುತ್ತಾರೆ	âḍa bâ annuttâre
They tell me to come to play	to play come they say
ಆಡಲಿಕ್ಕೆ ಕರೆಯುತ್ತಾರೆ	âḍalikke kareyuttâre
They call me to play	to play they call
ಈ ಆಟ ನಮಗೆ ಬರುವದಿಲ್ಲ	î âṭa namage baruvad' illa
We do not know this game	this play to us the coming is not

ಅವರ ಆಟ ಕೆಡಿಸ ಬೇಡ
Don't spoil their game
avara âṭa keḍisa bêḍa
their play to spoil is not wanted

ಯಾಕೆ ಹಾಕ್ಯಾಡಿದಿರಿ?
Why did you quarrel?
yâke hâkyâḍidiri[1]?
why you quarrelled?

ಹಾಕ್ಯಾಡಲಿಲ್ಲ, ಮಾತಾಡಿ ಕೊಂಡೆವು
We did not quarrel, we were talking together
hâkyâḍal'illa, mât'âḍi koṇḍevu
to quarrel is not, we talked

ನಿಮ್ಮನ್ನು ಕೊಂಡಾಡುತ್ತಿದ್ದೆವು
We were praising you
nimmannu koṇḍ' âḍutt' iddevu[2]
you h. taken playing we were

85. ಕಳುಹಿಸು kaḷuhisu = to send (*G. senden, schicken*).

ತಂಗಿಯನ್ನು ಕಳುಹಿಸಲಿಕ್ಕೆ ಬಂದೆ
I have accompanied my sister hither
taṅgiyannu kaḷuhisalikke bande
sister to send I came

ಯಾವಾಗ ಹಿಂದಕ್ಕೆ ಕಳುಹಿಸುತ್ತೀರಿ?
When will you send her back?
yâvâga hindakke kaḷuhisuttiri?
when back you send?

15 ದಿವಸದ ಮೇಲೆ ಕಳುಹಿಸ್ಯೇವು
Perhaps we shall send her after a fortnight
hadineidu divasada mêle kaḷuhisyêvu
15 of day after we may send

ಹಾಗಾದರೆ ಕರೇ ಕಳುಹಿಸ್ಯೇನು
Then I shall send for her
hâg' âdare karê[3] kaḷuhisyênu
thus if become to call I shall send

ನಮಗೆ ಕುದುರೆ ಕಳುಹಿಸಿ ಕೊಟ್ಟರು
They have sent us a horse
namage kudure kaḷuhisi koṭṭaru
to us horse h. sent they gave

ಅದನ್ನ ಹಿಂದಕ್ಕೆ ಕಳುಹಿಸ ಬೇಕು
It should be returned
adanna hindakke kaḷuhisa bêku
it back to send is wanted

ಕಳುಹಿಸೆಂತ ಬರೆದರು
They have written me to send it
kaḷuhis'enta baredaru
send saying they wrote

ಯಾವಾಗ ಕಳುಹಿಸಲಿ?
When shall I (a. p.) send it?
yâvâga kaḷuhisali?
when let (a. p.) send?

ಈಗ ಕಳುಹಿಸಿದರೆ ಆದೀತು
You may send it now
iga kaḷuhisidare âditu
now if sent it will do

[1] From *hâki + âḍu*, the final vowel *i* is changed into the consonant *y*; the compound word has the meaning of "to dispute, to quarrel"; "words" or "abuses" is to be understood as the object of *hâki*.

[2] From *koṇḍu + âḍu*: "your praise" or "your name" may be understood as the object of *koṇḍu*.

[3] *Karê*, infinitive for *kareya*.

ಎಂಟು ದಿವಸದ ಹಿಂದೆ ಕಳುಹಿಸಿ ಬಿಟ್ಟೆ	*yeṇṭu* **divasada hinde kaḷuhisi biṭṭe**
I sent it off a week ago	8 of day back h. sent I left

86. ಒಳ್ಳೇ *woḷḷê* = good (*G. gut*).

ಎಂಥಾ ಒಳ್ಳೇ ಹುಡುಗ!	*yenthâ* *woḷḷê* **huḍuga!**
What a nice boy!	what kind good boy!
ಹೌದು, ಬಹಳ ಒಳ್ಳೆಯವ	**houdu, bahaḷa** *woḷḷe*-**y-ava**
Yes, he is very nice	yes, very good one
ಅವರಣ್ಣ ಅಷ್ಟು ಒಳ್ಳೆಯವನಲ್ಲ	**avar'aṇṇa ashṭu** *woḷḷe*-**y-avan'alla**
His brother is not so nice	their elder brother so much good one [not
ಹೌದು, ಅಣ್ಣನಿಗಿಂತ ಇವನೇ ಒಳ್ಳೆಯವ	**houdu, aṇṇanig'inta ivanê** *woḷḷe*-**y-ava**
Yes, he is better than his brother	yes, than elder brother *he* good one
ಅಣ್ಣತಮ್ಮಂದಿರಲ್ಲಿ ಇವನೇ ಒಳ್ಳೆಯವ	**aṇṇatammandiralli**[1] **ivanê** *woḷḷe*-**y-ava**
He is the best of his brothers	in brothers *he* good one
ಅವನ ಮಾತು ಎಂಥಾ ಒಳ್ಳೇದು!	**avana mâtu** *yenthâ* *woḷḷêdu*!
How well he talks!	his word what kind of good!
ಒಳ್ಳೇದು, ಈ ಮಾತಿರಲಿ	*woḷḷêdu*, **i mât' irali**
Well, let this pass	good, this word let (*a. p.*) be
ಯಾವಾಗ ಬರೋಣಾಯಿತು?	**yâvâga barôṇ' âyitu?**
When did you arrive?	when the coming it became?
ಬಂದಾಗ ಒಳ್ಳೇ ರಾತ್ರಿ ಇತ್ತು	**band' âga** *woḷḷê* **râtri ittu**
It was quite dark when I came	come then good night it was
ಬಂದದ್ದು ಒಳ್ಳೇದಾಯಿತು	**bandaddu** *woḷḷêd'* **âyitu**
It is well that you are come	the h. come good one became

87. ಹೊಸ **hosa** = new (*G. neu*); ಹಳೇ **haḷê** = old (*G. alt*); ಹೊಸಬ **hosaba** = a new man; ಹಳಬ **haḷaba** = (an old man) a beadle, village-servant.

ಏ (ಓ *C.*) ಹಳಬಾ, ಊರಿನ ಮಂದಿ ಕರೆ	**ê (ô *C.*) haḷabâ, ûrina mandi kare**
Ho there, beadle, call the village people	ho old one, town's people call

[1] *Aṇṇatamma* is a compound word used only in the plural number and signifying "brothers"; it is, like *tâyitande* = parents, declined by adding the terminations to the last word, as *aṇṇatammandiru*, *tâyitandegaḷu*.

ಎಲ್ಲರು ಹೊಸಬರೋ? C. ಹೊಸಬರೇನು? S. — *y*ellaru hosabar'ô? C. hosabar' ênu? S.
Are they all new? ...new comers? — all new ones? new ones what?
ಕೆಲವರು ಹಳೇ ಮಂದಿ (ಹಳಬರು) — kelavaru haḷê mandi (haḷabaru)
Some are old (*i. e.* old comers) — some old people
ಈತನು ಹೊಸಬ — îtanu hosaba
This is a new man (...new comer) — he new one
ಆತನೂ ಹೊಸ್ತಾಗಿ ಬಂದವ — âtanû host'âgi[1] band'ava
That also is a new comer — he even newly one who came
ಇವನು ಹಳೇ ಊರಿನವ — ivanu haḷê ûrin' ava
This one is an inhabitant of the old town — this old town's he
ಆತ ಹೊಸಮನೇ ರಾಮಪ್ಪ — âta hosamanê[2] râmappa
This man is Râmappa Hosamane — that new house's Râmappa
ಆತನ ಮನೆ ಹೊಸಾದೇನು? S. ...ಹೊಸಾದೋ? C. — âtana mane hosâd'ênu[3]? S. ...hosâd'ô? C.
Is his house new? — his house new what? ...new?
ಮುಂಚೆ ಹೊಸಾದಿತ್ತು — muṅče hosâd' ittu
Formerly it was new — formerly new it was
ಈಗ ಹಳೇದಾಗಿದೆ — îga haḷêd' âgide
Now it has become old — now old one it has become

88. ದೊಡ್ಡ **doḍḍa** = great, tall, big (*G. gross*); ಸಣ್ಣ **saṇṇa**, ಚಿಕ್ಕ **čikka** = small, little, young (*G. klein*).

ಎಷ್ಟು ದೊಡ್ಡವನಾದಿ! — *y*eshṭu doḍḍ' avan' âdi!
How tall you have grown! — how much tall one thou becamest!
ಮುಂಚೆ ಬಹಳ ಸಣ್ಣವನಿದ್ದಿ — muṅče bahaḷa saṇṇ' avan' iddi
Formerly you were very small — formerly very small one thou wast
ಈ ದೊಡ್ಡ ಹುಡುಗಿ ನಿಮ್ಮಕ್ಕೇನು? S. ...ಅಕ್ಕನೋ? C. — î doḍḍa huḍugi nimm'akk'ênu? S. ...akkan'ô? C.
Is this tall girl your sister? — this tall girl your elder sister what? ...elder sister?

[1] For *hosatu âgi* = *hosadu âgi*, an adverb; the verbal participle *âgi*, when added to nouns or adjectives, gives them the force of adverbs.

[2] *Manê* = *maneya*; surnames are commonly placed first.

[3] The word *hosadu* is generally pronounced *hosâdu*.

ಈಕೆ ನಮ್ಮಕ್ಕ, ಆಕೆ ಚಿಗವ್ವ	ike namm' akka, âke čig'avva[1]
This is my sister, and that is my [aunt	this our elder sister, that little mother
ನಿಮ್ಮಕ್ಕ ಎಷ್ಟು ದೊಡ್ಡಾಕೆ!	nimm' akka *y*eshṭu doḍḍ' âke!
How tall your sister is!	your elder sister, how much tall one!
ಚಿಗವ್ವನಿಗಿಂತ ದೊಡ್ಡಾಕೆ	čig' avvanig'inta doḍḍ' âke
She is taller than your aunt	little than mother tall one
ಈತ ಚಿಗಪ್ಪನೇನು? S. ...ಚಿಗಪ್ಪನೋ? C.	ita čig' appan'ênu? S. ...čig'appan'ô? C.
Is this your junior uncle? (...father's younger brother?)	this little father what? ... little father?
ಚಿಗಪ್ಪನಲ್ಲ, ದೊಡ್ಡಪ್ಪ	čig' appan' alla, doḍḍ' appa
Not my junior but my senior uncle; (...my father's elder brother)	little father not, great father
ಇನ್ನೂ ಚಿಕ್ಕವನಾಗಿ ಕಾಣಿಸುತ್ತಾನೆ	innû čikk' avan' âgi kâṇisuttâne
He seems still young	still young one h. become he appears
ಅವರಿಗೆ ದೊಡ್ಡ ಮನೆಯದೆ	avarige doḍḍa mane-y-ade
He (*or pl.*) possesses a large house	to them great house it is

89. ತುಸ **tusa** *S., or* ಸ್ವಲ್ಪ **svalpa** *C.* (ಸ್ವಲ್ಪು **svalpu** *S.*) = little (*G. ein wenig*); ಬಹಳ **bahaḷa** = much, very, many; ಹೆಚ್ಚು **hečču**, *adj. or adv.* = much, more (*G. mehr*); *verb intr.* = to increase (*G. sich vermehren*).

ಒಂದು ತುಸ (ಸ್ವಲ್ಪ) ನೀರು ತಾ	*w*ondu tusa (svalpa) nîru tâ
Fetch me a little water	one little water bring
ತುಸ ತಂದಿದ್ದೇನೆ	tusa tand' iddhêne
I have brought some	little h. brought I am
ಇನ್ನೂ ಹೆಚ್ಚು ಬೇಕಾಗುತ್ತದೆ	innû hečču bêk' âguttade
I want more	still more is wanted
ಇನ್ನಷ್ಟು ತಾ *S. or* ಇನ್ನೂ ಸ್ವಲ್ಪ ತಾ *C.*	inn' ashṭu tâ *S. or* innû svalpa tâ *C.*
Bring a little more	still so much bring, still little bring
ಬಹಳ ಬೇಡ, ತುಸ (ಸ್ವಲ್ಪ *C.*) ತಾ	bahaḷa bêḍa, tusa (svalpa *C.*) tâ
I don't want much, bring a little	much is not wanted, little bring
ಈ ಹುಡುಗರಿಗೆ ತುಸ ತುಸ (ಸ್ವಲ್ಪ ಸ್ವಲ್ಪ) ಕೊಡು	i huḍugarige tusa tusa (svalpa svalpa) koḍu
Give a little to each of these boys	these to boys little little give

[1] Instead of *čikka avva*; that is, « one's mother's younger sister » or « one's father's younger brother's wife ».

ನಿಮ್ಮಲ್ಲಿ ಹುಡುಗರು ಬಹಳ	nimmalli huḍugaru bahaḷa
You have a great many boys	with you boys many
ಬಹಳ ಹುಡುಗರಿರುತ್ತಾರೆ	bahaḷa huḍugar' iruttâre
There are many boys	many boys are
ಮುಂಚೆ ಸ್ವಲ್ಪ ಮಂದಿ ಇದ್ದರು [(boys)	muńče svalpa mandi iddaru
Formerly there were only a few	formerly few people were
ಬರ ಬರುತ್ತಾ ಹೆಚ್ಚಾದರು [ed	bara baruttâ'[1] heččâdaru [came
Gradually the number has increas-	coming coming more people they be-

90. *The same continued.*

ಈ ಕುದುರೆಗೆಷ್ಟು ರೂಪಾಯಿ ಕೊಟ್ಟಿರಿ?	î kudureg' eshṭu rûpâyi koṭṭiri?
How much did you give for this horse?	this to horse how many rupee you gave?
ಬಹಳ ಕೊಟ್ಟೆ	bahaḷa koṭṭe
A great deal	much I gave
ನೂರಕ್ಕಿಂತ ಹೆಚ್ಚು ಕೊಟ್ಟೆ	nûrakkinta hečču koṭṭe
I gave more than a hundred rupees	than 100 more I gave
ಬಹಳಾಯಿತು	bahaḷ' âyitu
It is very much	much it became
ಅಷ್ಟು ಬಹಳ ಕೊಡ ಬಾರದಿತ್ತು [as that	ashṭu bahaḷa koḍa bârad' ittu [it was
You should not have given so much	so much more to give the not coming
ನಾನಾದರೆ ಐವತ್ತು ಕೊಡುತ್ತಿದ್ದೆ	nân' âdare eivattu koḍutt' idde
As for me, I should have given fifty	I if become 50 giving I was
ಹೆಚ್ಚು ಕೊಡುತ್ತಿದ್ದಿಲ್ಲ [that)	hečču koḍutt' idd' illa
I should not have given more (than	more giving h. been is not
ಕೆಲವರು ಮೇಲಾಡುತ್ತಿದ್ದರು	kelavaru mêl' âdutt' iddaru
Some people were out-bidding me	some above playing were
ಅದಕ್ಕೆ ಹೆಚ್ಚು ಕೊಡ ಬೇಕಾಯಿತು [more	adakke hečču koḍa bêk' âyitu
Therefore I was obliged to give	for that more to give was wanted
ಕೆಲವರು ತಮ್ಮನ್ನು ಬಹಳ ಹೆಚ್ಚಿಸಿಕೊಳ್ಳುತ್ತಾರೆ	kelavaru tammannu bahaḷa heččisi koḷḷuttâre
Some people are very arrogant (exalt themselves. Luke 14, 11.)	some themselves much h. increased they take

[1] Instead of *baruttâ baruttâ.*

91. ಕೆಲವು kelavu=some (*G. einige*).

ನಿಮ್ಮಣ್ಣ ಬಂದು ಎಷ್ಟು ದಿವಸವಾಯಿತು?	**nimm'aṇṇa bandu yeshṭu divasa-v-âyitu?**
How long is it since your brother arrived?	your elder brother h. come how many day it became?
ಕೆಲವು ದಿವಸಾದವು	**kelavu divas' âdavu**
A few days	some day they became
ಕೆಲವಂದರೆಷ್ಟು?	**kelav' andar' eshṭu?**
What do you mean by "a few"?	some if said how many?
ನಾಲ್ಕೈದು ದಿವಸ ಆಗಿದ್ದೀತು	**nâlk' eidu divasa âg' iddîtu**
It may be four or five days	four five day h. become it may be
ಕೆಲವು ಕುದುರೆಗಳನ್ನು ತಕ್ಕೊಂಡು ಬಂದ	**kelavu kuduregaḷannu takkoṇḍu banda**
He has brought some horses	some horses h. taken he came
ಯಾರಾದರೂ ಕುದುರೆ ತಕ್ಕೊಂಡರೇನು?	**yâr' âdarû kudure takkoṇḍar' ênu?**
Has any one bought some horses?	who if become even horse they took what?
ಕೆಲವರು ತಕ್ಕೊಂಡರು	**kelavaru takkoṇḍaru**
Some have bought [ಲ್ಲಿಲ್ಲ *C.*	some took [...iral'illa *C.*
ಕೆಲವರಿಗೆ ರೂಪಾಯಿ ಇದ್ದಿಲ್ಲ *S.*...ಇರ	**kelavarige rûpâyi idd'illa** *S.*
Some had no money	to some rupee h. been not, ..to be is not
ಕೆಲವರಿಂದ ರೂಪಾಯಿ ಇನ್ನೂ ಬಂದಿಲ್ಲ	**kelavarinda rûpâyi innû band'illa**
Some have not yet paid	from some rupee yet even h. come is not
ಕೆಲವರಲ್ಲಿ ರೂಪಾಯಿ ಇದ್ದರೂ ಕೊಡಲಿಲ್ಲ	**kelavaralli rûpâyi iddarû koḍal' illa**
Some have not paid, though they have the money	in some rupee if become even to give is not

92. ಇನ್ನು innu=yet, still (*G. noch*).

ನಿಮ್ಮಣ್ಣ ಇನ್ನೂ ಬಂದಿಲ್ಲಾ?	**nimm'aṇṇa innû band' illâ?**
Has your brother not yet arrived?	your elder brother yet even h. come is not?
ಇನ್ನೂ ಇಲ್ಲ, ಹಾಗಾದರೆ ಹೋಗುತ್ತೇನೆ	**innû illa, hâg' âdare hôguttêne**
Not yet, then I am going	yet even not, thus if become I go

ಹೋಗ ಬೇಡ, ಇನ್ನೂ ಇರು	**hôga bêḍa, innû iru**
Do not go, remain a little longer	to go is not wanted, yet be
ಇನ್ನು ಮೇಲೆ ಬಂದಾನು	**innu mele bandânu**
He will be coming now	yet after he may come
ರಾತ್ರಿ ಆಯಿತು ಇನ್ನು ಬರಲಿಕ್ಕಿಲ್ಲ	**râtri âyitu, innu baralikk'illa**
It is dark, he will not come now	night it became, yet to come is not
ಇನ್ನಾದರೂ ಬರ ಬಹುದು	**inn'âdarû bara bahudu**
He may still come	yet if become even to come it will come
ಇನ್ನೆಷ್ಟು ದಿವಸದೊಳಗೆ ಹೋಗುತ್ತಾನೆ?	**inn' eshṭu divasad' oḷage hôguttâne?**
Within how many days will he depart?	yet how many day's within he goes?
ಇನ್ನೆಂಟು ದಿವಸಾದ ಮೇಲೆ	**inn' eṇṭu divas' âda mêle**
After a week	yet 8 day after becoming
ನಿನಗಿನ್ನೊಬ್ಬ ಅಣ್ಣ ಇರುತ್ತಾನಲ್ಲಾ?	**ninag' inn' obba aṇṇa iruttân' allâ?**
You have yet another brother, have you not?	to you yet one elder brother is not?
ಇನ್ನಿಬ್ಬರಿರುತ್ತಾರೆ	**inn' ibbar' iruttâre**
I have two more	yet two are

93. ಹಿಂದೆ **hinde**=behind, formerly (*G. hinten, früher*);
ಮುಂದೆ **munde**=in front, in future (*G. vor, vorn, in Zukunft*);
ಮುಂಚೆ **muñce**=before, formerly (*G. vor, früher*). see Remark p. 9.

Cases still in use

Nom. **hindu**, the near, the back part
Instr. **hindininda**, from behind, from a former time
Dat. **hindakke**, behind, to a former time, at...
Gen. **hindina**, hind, former
Loc. **hinde**, behind, formerly

munde and muñce are declined in the same way.

ನಿನ್ನ ಕೆಲಸ ಹಿಂದು ಮುಂದೆ ಮಾಡಿದಿ	**ninna kelasa hindu munde maḍidi**
You have done your work in a confused way	thy work hind part in front thou didst
ಹಿಂದಕ್ಕೊಮ್ಮೆ ಆದರಂತೇ ಮಾಡಿದ್ದಿ	**hindakk'omme[1]adar'antê maḍiddi**
You had done the same once before	formerly once like *that* h. done thou wast

1 *Womme*, adverb derived from the numeral adjective *wondu*, signifying "once".

ಒಳ್ಳೇದು, ಹಿಂದಿನ ಮಾತಿರಲಿ	*wo*ḷḷêdu, hindina mât' irali
Well, let bygones be bygones	good, former word let be
ಇನ್ನು ಮುಂದೆ ಹೀಗೆ ಮಾಡ ಬೇಡ	innu munde hîge mâḍa bêḍa
In future never do so again	yet in future thus to do is not wanted
ಹಿಂದು ಮುಂದು ನೋಡಿ ಕೆಲಸ ಮಾಡು	hindu mundu nôḍi kelasa mâḍu
Do your work carefully (with circumspection)	hind part fore part h. seen work do
ಮುಂದಿನವರು ಹಿಂದಕ್ಕೆ ಹೋಗಲಿ	mundin' avaru hindakke hôgali
Let those in front go to the rear	those in front to the rear let go
ಹಿಂದಿನವರು ಮುಂದಕ್ಕೆ ಬರಲಿ	hindin' avaru mundakke barali
Let those behind come to the front	those of the rear to the front let come
ನನ್ನ ಮುಂದಿನಿಂದ ಹೋಗಿರಿ	nanna mundininda hôgiri
Go on before me	my from before go
ನಾನು ಹಿಂದೆ ಬರುತ್ತೇನೆ	nânu hinde baruttêne
I am going behind	I behind come
ಹಿಂದು ಮುಂದು ನೋಡಿಕೊಂಡು ಹೋಗಿರಿ	hindu mundu nôḍi koṇḍu hôgiri
Go along cautiously	rear front h. seen h. taken go

94. *The same continued.*

ನೀವು ಮುಂಚೆ ಈ ಊರಲ್ಲಿದ್ದಿರೇನು? S. ...ರೋ? C.	nivu muńče i ûrall' iddir' ênu? S. ...rô? C.
Have you been in this place [before?	you before this in town you were what?
ಇಲ್ಲ, ಹದಿನೈದು ದಿವಸದ ಹಿಂದೆ ಬಂದೆವು	illa, hadineidu divasada hinde bandevu
No, we arrived a fortnight ago	not, 15 of day behind we came
ಇಲ್ಲಿಗೆ ಬರುವದಕ್ಕಿಂತ ಮುಂಚೆ ಎಲ್ಲಿದ್ದಿರಿ?	illige baruvadakk'inta muńče *y*ell' iddiri?
Where did you live before you came here?	hither than the coming before where you were?
ಮುಂಚೆ ಮುಂಬಾಯಿಯಲ್ಲಿದ್ದೆವು	muńče mumbâyiyall' iddevu
Formerly we lived in Bombay	before in Bombay we were
ಅದಕ್ಕೂ ಮುಂಚೆ ಮಂಗಳೂರಲ್ಲಿ	adakkû muńče maṅgaḷûralli
And before that at Mangalore	to that even before in Mangalore
ಮುಂದೆ ಏನು ಮಾಡುವಿರಿ?	munde *y*ênu mâḍuviri?
What are you going to do in future?	in future what you will do?
ಹಿಂದಿನ ಮಾತು ಹೇಳಿದೆವು	hindina mâtu hêḷidevu
We have told you the past	former word we told

ಆದರೆ ಮುಂದಿನದು ಯಾರಿಗೆ ಗೊತ್ತು?	**âdare mundin'adu yârige gottu?**
But who knows the future?	**but of the future that to whom certainty?**
ನಮ್ಮ ಮುಂದೆ ಇಂಥಾ ಮಾತು ಆಡ ಬೇಡ	**namma munde inthâ mâtu âḍa bêḍa**
Do not talk like this in my presence	**our before such word to play not wanted**
ಇನ್ನು ಮುಂದೆ ಹೀಗೆ ಮಾಡುವದಿಲ್ಲ	**innu munde hige mâḍuvad' illa**
In future I shall never do so	**yet in future thus the doing is not**

95. ಹೊರಗೆ **horage** = out, without, outside (*G. aussen hinaus, ausser*); ಒಳಗೆ ***wo*ḷage** = in, within, inside (*G. innen, innerhalb, hinein, in*).

Cases in use.

Nom. **horagu, the outside.**
Instr. **horagininda, from the outside.**
Dat. **horage, horakke, to the outside, out.**
Gen. **horagina, horagaṇa, outer, external.**
Loc. **horage, horaginalli, on the outside.**
***wo*ḷage, follows the same rule.**
***wo*ḷagâgu = to obey.**

ನಿಮ್ಮ ಮಗ ಒಳಗಿದ್ದಾನೇನು? *S.* ...ನೋ? *C.*	**nimma maga *wo*ḷag' iddhân' ênu?** *S.* **...nô?** *C.*
Is your son inside?	**your son within he is what? ...is?**
ಮನೆಯೊಳಗಿಲ್ಲ	**maney'oḷag' illa**
He is not at home	**house within he is not**
ಹೊರಗೆ ಹೋಗಿದ್ದಾನೆ.	**horage hôg' iddhâne**
He has gone out	**outside h. gone he is**
ಸ್ವಲ್ಪ ಹೊತ್ತಿನೊಳಗೆ ಬಂದಾನು	**svalpa hottin' oḷage bandânu**
He may come within a short time	**little of time within he may come**
ಅವನು ಬರುವಷ್ಟರೊಳಗೆ ನಮ್ಮ ಮನೆ ನೋಡ ಬರ್ರಿ	**avanu baruv'ashṭar'oḷage namma mane nôḍa barri**
Come to have a look at my house till he return	**he coming of so much within our house to see come**
ಇವನ ಹೊರಗಿನ ಮಾತು ಚಲೋದು	**ivana horagina mâtu ćalôdu**
His outside (his words) is very fine	**his outer word fine one**
ಒಳಗಿನದು ಮಾತ್ರ ಕೆಟ್ಟದ್ದು	***wo*ḷaginadu mâtra keṭṭaddu**
But his inside is very bad	**inner one only bad one**

ಅವನು ಒಳಗೊಂದು ಹೊರಗೊಂದು	avanu **wo**ḷag' ondu horag' ondu
He is a hypocrite	he inside one outside one
ತಾಯಿತಂದೆಗಳಿಗೆ ಒಳಗಾಗುವದಿಲ್ಲ	tâyitandegaḷige **wo**ḷag' âguvad'illa
He is disobedient to his parents	to parents the obeying is not
ಅವನ ಕೆಟ್ಟ ಕೆಲಸ ಹೊರಬಿದ್ದೀತು	avana keṭṭa kelasa hora[1] biddîtu
His wickedness will come to light	his bad work out may fall

96. ಹತ್ತರ hattara = near (*G. nahe*).

Declined like **kelasa** No. 22.

ಇವರ ಮನೆ ಎಲ್ಲಿ ಅದೆ?	ivara mane *y*elli ade?
Where is his house?	their house where is?
ಹತ್ತರದೆ (ಹತ್ತರವದೆ), ದೂರಿಲ್ಲ	hattar' ade (hattara-v-ade), dûr'illa
It is not far, it is quite near	near it is, far is not
ನಮ್ಮ ಮನೇ ಹತ್ತರ	namma manê[2] hattara
It is near my house	our house's near
ಆಗಾಗ್ಗೆ ನಿಮ್ಮ ಹತ್ತರ ಬರುತ್ತಿರುತ್ತಾನೇನು?	âg'âgge nimma hattara barutt'iruttân'ênu?
Does he visit you now and then	then then your near coming he is what?
ನಮ್ಮ ಹತ್ತರ ಬರುವದಿಲ್ಲ	namma hattara baruvad' illa
He does not visit us (me)	our near the coming is not
ನಾನು ಅವನ ಹತ್ತರ ಹೋಗುವದಿಲ್ಲ	nânu avana hattara hôguvad' illa
I do not visit him	I his near the going is not
ಬಾ, ತಮ್ಮಾ, ಹತ್ತರ ಬಾ	bà, tammâ, hattara bâ
Come here, little boy, come near	come, younger brother, near come
ನಿನ್ನ ಹತ್ತರ ಒಂದು ರೂಪಾಯಿ ಅದೇನು?	ninna hattara *w*ondu rûpâyi ad' ênu?
Have you got a rupee with you?	your near one rupee is what?
ನನ್ನ ಹತ್ತರ ಏನೂ ಇಲ್ಲ	nanna hattara *y*ênû illa
I have not got anything (any money)	my near what even is not
ಇವರ ಹತ್ತರ ರೂಪಾಯಿ ಇದ್ದಾವು	ivara hattara rûpâyi iddâvu
This person (*or pl.*) may perhaps have some money	their near rupee they may be

97. ತನಕ tanaka = till, as far as (*G. bis*).

ನಿಮ್ಮ ಹಿಂದೆ ಬರುತ್ತೇನೆ	nimma hinde baruttêne
I am following you	your behind I come

[1] Instead of *horage.*

[2] Instead of *maneya.*

ಎಲ್ಲಿ ತನಕ ಬರುತ್ತೀರಿ?	yelli tanaka baruttîri?
How far will you come?	where as far as you come?
ನಿಮ್ಮ ಮನೇ ತನಕ ಬರುತ್ತೇನೆ	nimma manê tanaka baruttêne
As far as your house	your house's as far as I come
ಮುಂಬಾಯೀ ತನಕ	mumbâyî tanaka
As far as Bombay	of Bombay as far as
ಮುಂಬಾಯಿ ಮುಂಚೆ ನೋಡಿದ್ದಿಲ್ಲೇನು? *S.* ...ಲ್ಲವೋ? *C.*	mumbâyi muñce nôḍ' idd' ill' ênu? *S*....illavô? *C*.
Have you never seen Bombay yet?	Bombay before h. seen h. been is not what?
ಇಂದಿನ ತನಕ ನೋಡಿದ್ದಿಲ್ಲ	indina tanaka nôḍ' idd' illa
I have never seen it up to this day	to-day's till h. seen h. been I am not
ಇಲ್ಲೀ ತನಕ ನಮ್ಮೂರು ಬಿಡಲಿಲ್ಲ	illî tanaka namm' ûru biḍal' illa
I never left my native town till now	of here till our town to leave is not
ಹಾಗಾದರೆ ಅಲ್ಲೀ ತನಕ ಬರ್ರಿ	hâg'âdare allî tanaka barri
Then come as far as that	thus if become of there as far as come
ನಾ ಬರುವ ತನಕ ಹೋಗ ಬೇಡಿರಿ	nâ baruva tanaka hôga bêḍiri
Do not go before I come	I coming till to go is not wanted
ನೀವು ಬರುವ ತನಕ ನಿಂತಿರುತ್ತೇನೆ	nîvu baruva tanaka nint' iruttêne
I shall stay till you come	you coming till h. stood I am

98. ಮಾತ್ರ mâtra = only (*G. nur*).

ಎಷ್ಟು ಮಂದಿಗೆ ಉಣ್ಣಲಿಕ್ಕೆ ಹೇಳಿದ್ದಿರಿ?	yeshṭu mandige uṇṇalikke hêḷ' iddiri?
How many people had you invited to dinner?	how many to people to eat h. told you were?
ಮೂವತ್ತು ಮಂದಿಗೆ ಮಾತ್ರ ಹೇಳಿದ್ದೆವು	mûvattu mandige mâtra hêḷ' iddevu
We had invited only 30 people	30 to people only h. told we were
ಇಪ್ಪತ್ತು ಮಂದಿ ಮಾತ್ರ ಬಂದಿದ್ದರು	ippattu mandi mâtra band' iddaru
Only 20 people had come	20 people only h. come were
ನಿಮ್ಮ ಮನೆಯವರು ಬಂದಿದ್ದರು	nimma maney' avaru band' iddaru
Your family had come	your house's they h. come were
ನಿಮ್ಮನ್ನು ಮಾತ್ರ ನೋಡಲಿಲ್ಲ	nimmannu mâtra nôḍal' illa
You only I did not see	you only to see is not
ನೀವು ಮಾತ್ರ ಬಂದಿದ್ದಿಲ್ಲ	nîvu mâtra band' idd' illa
You only were not come	you only h. come h. been are not

ಎಷ್ಟು ಘಂಟೇ ತನಕಿದ್ದರು?	**yeshṭu ghaṇṭê tanak' iddaru?**
How long did people remain?	how many of the bell till they were?
ಹತ್ತು ಘಂಟೇ ತನಕ ಮಾತ್ರ ಇದ್ದರು	**hattu ghaṇṭê tanaka mâtra iddaru**
Only till 10 o'clock	10 of the bell till only they were
ಕೆಲವರು ಹನ್ನೆರಡು ಘಂಟೇ ತನಕ ಇದ್ದರಂತೆ	**kelavaru hanneraḍu ghaṇṭê tanaka iddar' ante**
I heard that some remained till 12 o'clock	some 12 of the bell till they were it says
ನಾ ಮಾತ್ರ ನೋಡಲಿಲ್ಲ	**nâ mâtra nôḍal' illa**
I did not see them though	I only to see is not

96. ಒಂದು ***wondu***, ಒಬ್ಬ ***wobba*** = one (*G. ein*);

ಎರಡು ***yeraḍu***, ಇಬ್ಬರು **ibbaru** = two (*G. zwei*); **and other numerals.**

Wondu, *yeraḍu* and other numeral adjectives of the neuter gender are declined like adu, see No. 6, *wobba* follows ava; ibbaru, mûvaru etc. follow the pronoun avaru in declension.

When neuter numeral adjectives are to be used before nouns of the masculine or feminine gender, the word mandi is inserted.

ಎಷ್ಟು ಮಂದಿಯನ್ನು ಊಟಕ್ಕೆ ಕರೆಯಲಿ?	**yeshṭu mandiyannu ûṭakke kareyali?**
How many persons shall I invite to dinner?	how many people to dinner let (*a.p.*) call?
ಎಂಟು ಮಂದಿ ಕರೆ	**yeṇṭu mandi kare**
Invite eight persons	eight people call
ಇಬ್ಬರನ್ನು ಕರೆದೆ	**ibbarannu karede**
I have invited two	two I called
ಒಬ್ಬಿಬ್ಬರು ಮನೆಯಲ್ಲಿದ್ದಿಲ್ಲ	**wobb' ibbaru maneyall' idd' illa**
One or two were not at home	one two in the house h. been are not
ಒಬ್ಬನು ತಾ ಬರುವದಿಲ್ಲ ಅಂದ	**wobbanu tâ baruvad' illa anda**
One refused to come	one himself the coming is not he said
ಇನ್ನೂ ಒಬ್ಬಿಬ್ಬರಿಗೆ ಹೇಳ ಬೇಕು	**innû wobb' ibbarige hêḷa bêku**
One or two are still to be invited	still even to one to two to tell is wanted
ಇನ್ನೂ ಮೂರು ಮಂದಿಗ್ಹೇಳು	**innû mûru mandig[1] hêḷu**
Invite three persons more	still even three to people tell
ಈಗ ಎಂಟು ಮಂದಿ ಬಂದಿದ್ದಾರೆ	**îga yeṇṭu mandi band' iddâre**
Eight persons are come now	now eight people h. come are

ಇಬ್ಬರು ಹುಡುಗರಾದರೂ ಬಂದಿದ್ದಾರೆ	**ibbaru huḍugar' âdarû band'-iddâre**
Two boys also are come	two boys if become even h. come are
ಹಾಗೂ ಒಬ್ಬ ಹುಡುಗಿ	**hâgû *w*obba huḍugi**
A girl also	so even one girl

100. *The same continued.*

ಒಬ್ಬೊಬ್ಬರಿಗೆ ಎರಡೆರಡು ರೂಪಾಯಿ ಕೊಡುತ್ತೇನೆ	***w*obb' obbarige *y*eraḍ' eraḍu rûpâyi koḍuttêne**
I shall give them two rupees each	to one one two two rupee I give
ಒಂದೊಂದು ಕೊಡು	***w*ond' ondu koḍu**
Give each of them one	one one give
ಒಬ್ಬರ ಹಿಂದೊಬ್ಬರು ಹೋಗುತ್ತಾರೆ	***w*obbara hind'obbaru hôguttâre**
They are going one after the other	behind ones' ones they go
ಒಬ್ಬರಿಗೊಬ್ಬರು ಸಲಾಂಮಾಡಿಹೋದರು	***w*obbarig' obbaru salâm mâḍi hôdaru**
They went away saluting one another	to ones ones salâm h. made they went
ಇವರಿಬ್ಬರು ಅಣ್ಣ ತಮ್ಮಂದಿರು	**ivar' ibbaru aṇṇa tammandiru**
These two men are brothers	they two e. brother y. brothers
ಅವರ ಮನೆಗಳು ಒಂದಕ್ಕೊಂದು ದೂರವಾಗಿಲ್ಲ	**avara manegaḷu *w*ondakk' ondu dû-ra-v'âg'illa**
Their houses are not far from one another	their houses to one one far h. become are not
ಆದರೂ ಒಬ್ಬರ ಮನೆಗೊಬ್ಬರು ಹೋಗುವದಿಲ್ಲ	**âdarû *w*obbara maneg' obbaru hôgu-vad'illa**
But they do not visit one another	but even of the one (*pl.*) to house ones the going is not
ಒಬ್ಬರನ್ನೊಬ್ಬರು ಕರೆಯುವದಿಲ್ಲ	***w*obbarann' obbaru kareyuvad'illa**
They do not invite one another	ones (*acc.*) ones the calling is not
ಒಬ್ಬರಲ್ಲೊಬ್ಬರು ಊಟಮಾಡುವದಿಲ್ಲ	***w*obbarall' obbaru ûṭa mâḍuvad' illa**
They do not eat with one another	in ones ones meal the making is not
ಒಬ್ಬೊಬ್ಬನು ತನ್ನ ತನ್ನಷ್ಟಕ್ಕೆ ತಾನೇ ಇರುತ್ತಾನೆ	***w*obb' obbanu tanna tann' ashṭa-kke tânê iruttâne**
Each one remains for himself	one one his his to so much himself is